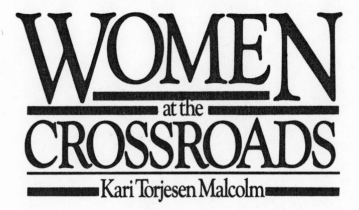

# WOMEN at the CROSSROADS

### Kari Torjesen Malcolm

A Path beyond
Feminism
and Traditionalism

InterVarsity Press
Downers Grove
Illinois 60515

InterVarsity Press is the book-publishing division of Inter-Varsity Christian Fellowship, a student movement active on campus at hundreds of universities, colleges and schools of nursing. For information about local and regional activities, write IVCF, 233 Langdon St., Madison, WI 53703.

Distributed in Canada through InterVarsity Press, 1875 Leslie St., Unit 10, Don Mills, Ontario M3B 2M5, Canada.

All quotations from the Scripture, unless otherwise noted, are from the Holy Bible: New International Version. Copyright © 1978 by the New York International Bible Society. Used by permission of Zondervan Bible Publishers.

ISBN 0-87784-379-1

Printed in the United States of America

**Library of Congress Cataloging in Publication Data**
Malcolm, Kari Torjesen, 1925-
    Women at the crossroads.

    Includes bibliographical references.
    1. Women (Christian theology)  2. Women in
Christianity.  3. Malcolm, Kari Torjesen,
1925-     .  I. Title.
BT704.M34              248.8'43              82-7228
ISBN 0-87784-379-1                          AACR2

17  16  15  14  13  12  11  10
95  94  93  92  91  90  89

To the man I love
Bob
my carpenter-farmer-minister husband
who is always ready
to make way for the other
Carpenter
who claims my first love

# Acknowledgments

Giving birth to a first book is much like having a first baby. My husband played a major role in both productions. Before Bob, my mother had her input in this book. First, she was my model for Christian womanhood. Then, shortly before her death, in her last complete letter to me, she wrote two pages suggesting that I start writing to communicate the good news. Encouragement has also come from her granddaughters, my daughters, Kirsten and Lois Ellen.

Beyond family, the most unexpected stimulus came from Dr. Allen Simpson of the University of Minnesota. After returning from the Philippines, I went back to graduate school and was discussing the possibility of pursuing an advanced degree. Dr. Simpson said, "With all your background, why don't you write?" I took that as a call from God.

Within a year I knew I was supposed to write about women, but how should I start? In answer to prayer for direction, God led me to well-known author Ruth Peterman and her classes in writing for publication. Ruth has become my mentor and trusted friend through the years that have followed and has faithfully corrected this manuscript.

Others have also helped with their critical chapter-by-chapter evaluation. Sally Harris, a former colleague from Northwestern College, has lent me her logical mind and given of her time unstintingly during a heavy Ph.D. program. The Rev. Irene Gifford, deacon of the Episcopal Church and a licensed psychologist, has helped with applying truth to life situations. Alvera Mickelsen of Bethel College (Journalism) came to my aid as a friend in a time of extreme discouragement. And Cathie Kroeger generously shared with me her understanding of New Testament times from her studies in classics.

Also a thousand thanks go to Eleanor Hulting Williams, Bob's cousin, for typing the whole manuscript as an act of love. And thanks go to the women who have prayed for me daily. They have been the midwives laboring with me to give birth to this book. How I thank God for them and others I have not named who have given practical help! More than having a baby, writing a book is a family affair within the context of the family of God.

# CHAPTER ONE

# Introduction

TOWERING NINE THOUsand feet above the seaport of Davao, Mount Apo was a favorite site during the fifteen years my husband and I were missionaries to the Philippines. On clear days the beautiful peak would lift our spirits, and on special holidays it would call us to drive the dusty, rocky road up its mountainside to escape the sultry heat below.

The first few times we tried to climb that peak we were thwarted. Our sturdy jeep puffed and choked uphill till we came to a T intersection where, we thought, we had to turn either left or right. Then one day we discovered a footpath going straight ahead almost hidden by the brush. We could park our jeep near the intersection and continue by foot directly up the mountain where cool breezes and a magnificent view of Davao Bay awaited us.

To me that crossroads has become symbolic of the choices available to Christian women today. I can look back to a time when I thought there were only two choices open to us—the road marked Tradition and the one named Rebellion. These choices spawned two popular movements, each with its slogans: "A woman's place is in the home" or "A woman's place is in the House and the Senate." Both groups look to certain roles to give women their identity. But what about the deeper problems of self-worth that every human being faces?

Jesus came to give an answer to all people struggling to find their identity. That's why at the start of his ministry, he read in the synagogue from Isaiah 61: "The Spirit of the Lord is on me, because he has anointed me to preach good news to the poor. He has sent me to proclaim freedom for the prisoners and recovery of sight for the blind, to release the oppressed, to proclaim the year of the Lord's favor" (Lk 4:18-19). Somehow the answers that the traditionalists and the secular feminists have given to the problem of woman's identity have never seemed to mesh with Christ's answer of release and liberation.

### The Feminists

According to the rules of many feminists, a woman must find her role in some meaningful vocation. Her career becomes the panacea for most of the ills mentioned in Isaiah 61 and Luke 4. It allows her to get away from the captivity of husband, children and home so that she can become a candidate for liberation in a world that promises fulfillment.

And why not? Haven't men too long enjoyed the monopoly on meaningful occupations outside the home? As Paul Goodman wrote, "Having a vocation is always something of a miracle, like falling in love. . . . I can understand why Luther said that a man is justified by his vocation, for it is already a proof of God's favor."[1]

So why, the feminists ask, shouldn't women also enjoy God's favor and be justified by their vocation? With the aid of science to reduce the distinctions between male and female to their basic minimum, women all over the world have set out to prove that given the same training and conditioning, men and women are usually able to do the same work.

In this effort, the married woman has two hurdles to overcome: gracefully leaving her home to go to work and tactfully entering the job market to compete with men. She often feels like an actor in the great drama of life. As a woman, she perceives herself as a victim of an unjust system. The bad guys are the men who have propagated the system throughout the ages. Since she is married to one of them and may have given birth to more, she must start at home to announce her rights as a woman. Many how-to books address these problems.

At first the woman who listens to the feminists is assured that every woman has a right—if that is what she wants— to find fulfillment in a meaningful vocation outside the home. But what if domestic conflict arises over such a proposition? One woman I knew believed that when the family made a fuss about it—as if the smooth running of the home were the woman's sole responsibility—then she had a right to leave permanently. And she did!

I met two other women caught in such domestic conflicts when I was in the United States for the summer of 1970. While attending an international gathering of five thousand women at Purdue University, a friend from the Philippines introduced me to some American feminists. We sat on bunk beds in our dormitory room and swapped tales of domestic life far into the night. One of the women—attractive, round and motherly—showed deep hostility toward men in general, while trying her best to defend her husband and exempt him from her complaints against the sex. The second woman was a more dependent type. Worry wrinkles sneaked in on her pretty face as she unloaded her deep bitterness against the man she had married. He had become the symbol of everything that had gone wrong in her life.

I listened. And I asked questions. Finally, I went to bed deeply disturbed. When I returned to the United States four years later, I asked what had happened to the two women. I was saddened to hear that they had left their families and moved in together.

Gail Sheehy documents a number of similar case histories in her book *Passages.* "Since we've divorced, she has changed," one man tells Sheehy after rehearsing how miserable his wife had been "not having made something of her life." Sheehy goes on: "After hearing that comment over and over again from men, I began to wonder if divorce is a *rite de passage.* Is this ritual necessary before anyone, above all herself, will take a woman's need for expansion seriously? The Changed Woman after divorce was a familiar figure to come out of the biographies, a dynamic figure, and one who usually held considerable allure for her startled former husband."[2]

Another of Sheehy's case histories, Melissa (thirty-five and trying desperately to avoid divorce) asked the burning question, "How does a woman find her identity outside of marriage without jeopardizing it or her children? I really don't know a woman my age who isn't going through this right now."[3]

Melissa stood at the crossroads. She admitted she was fearful—fearful of the havoc that might result if she allowed a role outside the home to determine her identity. Having watched some of her friends make idols out of their careers, she also saw them lose their families. Old structures of family life had been broken before new structures were formed. Melissa looked on and was immobilized with fear. There was no solution, she decided.

## The Traditionalists

The antifeminists do not give us a different image of women in conflict; they merely cheer for the opposing team. Melissa, at home, fighting desires for expansion, is the heroine. The traditionalists, like the feminists, focus on certain *roles* that women should fill. But the stereotypes in the traditional Christian community may produce results as sad as Sheehy's case histories. Mabel and her husband, Carl, are a model couple whose home is always open to the spiritually hungry, the jobless and the emotionally disturbed. Many young people who have never known a Christian home before have lived with Mabel and Carl for as long as a year at a time. In addition, each week an assortment of young and old meet at their home for praise, Bible study and sharing.

Eager to improve their effectiveness, Mabel and Carl went to a retreat where they opened themselves up for guidance from other Christians. Could there be an expansion in their witness? Mabel says that what happened was the same thing that occurred every time she and Carl asked for counsel from other Christians. One fellow suggested that the way Mabel expresses herself so freely is a threat to Carl.

"When two horses are yoked together, the faster one has to slow down," he concluded, as others chimed in about the necessity of Mabel's putting the brakes on so that Carl could develop as a leader. Mabel told me that after the retreat, Carl said again, as he had on numerous occasions, that he was not threatened by her being more vocal in meetings than he was.

"Why do they always have to harp on this?" Carl asked. "Why do people have to create a problem between mates in

an area where they don't have one?" Is it because other
men, not her husband, are threatened by her prophetic
role in a meeting?

## A Third Way

This traditionalism and the secular feminism of recent
years are the two roads familiar to most women. But I see
Christ offering us a third way—the way of love—as he calls
us to walk straight ahead with him up the mountain. It's
a different path, but it is the answer to the dilemma the
modern woman faces.

My purpose here is to look at that answer and proclaim
the good news that a woman finds her identity in her love
relationship with Jesus Christ. I believe that is what Scripture teaches. As we examine the relevant Scriptures together, you will find that at points I have changed the masculine pronouns used to address the readers of Scripture to
feminine. I am speaking to women in this book, and it is my
hope that changing the pronouns will help them apply
Scripture more directly to their lives. Each time these
changes are made they are indicated as my changes in
parentheses.

We will also look at our lives today and how the world
and the church, in some cases, have sought to define our
roles apart from our relationship to and our mission for the
Lord Jesus Christ. Because my own story illustrates this
truth, I will tell a bit of it along with the stories of other
women throughout history, from New Testament times to
the present. All of us have struggled with this issue of identity. We will see how this third way between traditionalism
and feminism affects our lives as single or married women,
at home, in society and around the world.

While none of us can ultimately understand another
woman's experiences completely, or find her identity for
her, I hope that many women will find their own stories

among the stories of others related here.

C. S. Lewis talks about stories in *The Horse and His Boy*. The young boy Shasta meets Aslan, the great Lion who rules the land of Narnia, and asks about a special friend of his. Aslan, who is hidden in a mist, replies:

"Child, . . . I am telling you your story, not hers. I tell no-one any story but his own."

"Who *are* you?" asked Shasta.

"Myself," said the Voice, very deep and low so that the earth shook: and again "Myself," loud and clear and gay: and then the third time "Myself," whispered so softly you could hardly hear it, and yet it seemed to come from all round you as if the leaves rustled with it. . . .

Shasta turned and saw, pacing beside him, taller than [Shasta's] horse, a Lion. . . . No-one ever saw anything more terrible or beautiful. . . . After one glance at the Lion's face he slipped out of the saddle and fell at its feet. . . .

The High King above all kings stooped towards him. . . . It touched his forehead with its tongue. He lifted his face and their eyes met. Then instantly the pale brightness of the mist and the fiery brightness of the Lion rolled themselves together into a swirling glory and gathered themselves up and disappeared.[4]

As each of us meets the Lion at the crossroads, we will find the way up the mountain. And we will hear our stories from our Lord's perspective and bow in worship and adoration before the One who is our first love.

# PART ONE

# "Nobody Knows the Trouble . . ."

# CHAPTER TWO

# The Great Escape

I FACED MY FIRST IDENTI-
ty crisis as a teen-ager in a concentration camp in China
during World War 2. "Who am I?" I wondered. "Number
16 among the prisoners who line up for roll call twice a
day?" Where did I belong?

Our homes had been confiscated, and our bank accounts
closed. Gone were all the things we thought were our birth-
right: our education, three square meals a day and our privacy. Even our beds were gone. Our world had been re-
duced to a space on the floor of a room. The enemy had
taken everything and given us a wall with electrified barbed
wire and a deep moat—constant reminders that we were
prisoners.

It was during our second year in prison camp that my
good friend Debbie decided to organize a prayer group.

Some of us teen-agers who had gone to school together before internment got permission from the guards to climb the bell tower every day at noon for our rendezvous. As we met to pray, only one type of prayer was voiced, "Lord, get us out of here!"

I also tried to pray on my own. Sometimes I would stand on a mound by the wall where I could look out on the green fields beyond the prison. There were times when I wondered if there really was a world beyond—or a God. I would pray fervently, "Lord, if you are there, please let me know. Please reveal yourself to me."

God answered that prayer and spoke to me as I searched the Bible for answers. Gradually it dawned on me that there was just one thing the enemy could not take from me. They had bombed our home, killed my father, and put my mother, brothers and me into prison. But the one thing they could not touch was my relationship to my God.

With this new discovery, it became more and more difficult to join the gang in prayer at noon. There was more to life than just getting out of prison. One day, I decided I could not climb the bell tower. It was the first time I had missed.

Debbie looked for me right after the meeting. The spot where we met is riveted in my memory. I cannot even remember trying to defend myself, but Debbie must have surmised something of what had occurred in my thinking. Her reproof ended with the final taunt, "So we aren't good enough for you anymore, eh? Getting holier than the rest of us, I can see."

As I walked away, I felt lonelier than I had ever felt in my life. My last bit of security was peeled off. This was the climax to the peeling process that had been going on through the war years with the loss of my father, my home, my education, my freedom. Now I no longer belonged to my peer group.

It was only then that I was able to pray the prayer that changed my life: "Lord, I am willing to stay in this prison for the rest of my life if only I may know You." At that moment I was free.

## The Narrow Path

Looking back, I am grateful for the three years of concentration camp, for it was there that God gave me my identity as his disciple, loved by him regardless of circumstances. Nothing could separate me from that love.

"That was your mount of transfiguration," remarked an Episcopal minister when I told him the story. He was right. That was the time in my life, above all others, when I discovered my first love.

It is in that discovery that the key to a woman's identity lies. If women search for their identity in roles, they make idols of those roles, of their careers, their homes, their children or husbands. None of these things and none of these roles can give women what they are searching for. It is only on the narrow path up the mountain, only in a first-love relationship with Jesus Christ that a woman will find what she seeks.

As a Norwegian brought up in China, married to an American and having spent many years in the Philippines, I have talked to a variety of Christian women about this search. The majority, regardless of culture, can look back on a time when their love relationship with Jesus Christ was so real that they found their complete identity in it. They expressed that love in worship.

Then what happened? Other interests and individuals came into competition with that primary commitment. Or perhaps the Christian church tried to push them into molds they did not fit—and they rebelled. After my initial discovery of Christ's love in prison, I too drifted away. My love cooled within me as ideas, people, organizations and movements competed for my attention.

Each time something replaces the love for Christ within us, inner conflict results. With this conflict comes a sense of failure and unfaithfulness to Jesus Christ and to ourselves, our dreams and ideals. There follows a feeling of hopelessness and a very low self-image.

I believe the answer to this cooling off is the one given by the apostle John to the church at Ephesus:

I know your deeds, your hard work and your perseverance. I know that you cannot tolerate wicked men, that you have tested those who claim to be apostles but are not, and have found them false. You have persevered and have endured hardships for my name, and have not grown weary.

Yet I hold this against you: *You have forsaken your first love. Remember* the height from which you have fallen! *Repent* and *do the things you did at first.* If you do not repent, I will come to you and remove your lampstand from its place. . . . She who has an ear, let her hear what the Spirit says to the churches. To her who overcomes, I will give the right to eat from the tree of life, which is in the paradise of God. (Rev 2:2-7, my changes)

**Culture Shock**
When women forget their love for Christ, then they allow culture and peer pressure to determine their identity.

I arrived in the U.S. for the first time in 1946 when I came to attend Wheaton College in Illinois. Culture shock hit in my very first class—speech. By the second day of class, students began giving practice speeches. To my amazement one day a young war veteran got up and proclaimed that women were going to college with the primary motivation of looking for husbands!

After years of waiting in prison to study at this particular Christian college to prepare for Christian service, I was being told in a public speech that my sense of destiny as a handmaid of the Lord was just a front for husband-hunting. What crushed me most was that nobody else in the room was bothered by the speech. They thought it was a big joke, while to me it touched on deep issues involving my identity as a disciple of Jesus Christ.

By the next day when it was my turn to give a speech, I was boiling with anger that such views were acceptable in a Christian college. With my British accent sounding tarter than usual, I replied in words that I am now sure were somewhat less than charitable.

Gradually and painfully, I discovered that my GI friend had been right on target in his analysis of why many women were in college. But I didn't understand that until years later when I read *The Feminine Mystique*. Betty Friedan describes how the feminine mystique was in full bloom right after World War 2. While I realize that Betty Friedan's name turns on red lights for many evangelicals, I wonder if we can listen to her as we might listen to a weather forecaster whose views on God would be unacceptable to us. Like the weather forecaster, Betty Friedan has done her homework. In her book she writes about the postwar mood I encountered on my arrival in the U.S.:

> Over and over women heard in voices of tradition and Freudian sophistication that they could desire no greater destiny than to glory in their own femininity. Experts told them how to catch a man and keep him, how to breastfeed children and handle their toilet training ... how to bake bread, cook gourmet snails ... and act more feminine and make marriage more exciting. ... They learned that truly feminine women do not want careers, higher education, political rights—the independence and the opportunities that the old-fashioned feminists fought for.[1]

Back at Wheaton, I couldn't understand why some of the

women I knew were so ambiguous about the careers they were preparing for—as if they were not planning to stay in them very long. Others had no interest in choosing careers at all, but settled for major fields in which they were only vaguely interested. Later I found out that in American high schools there was often more talk about choosing silver patterns and dinnerware than choosing careers. While reading for high-school women in the school in Chefoo, China, founded by Hudson Taylor in 1881 included *Careers for Girls,* women's magazines in the United States "urged that courses on marriage, and marriage counselors, be installed in the high schools."[2]

Among my friends at Wheaton was a vibrant woman who decided against medical school and the mission field when a man came into her life. It seemed as if the child within her—her dreams and aspirations of many years—had died. Somehow the vision of serving Christ as a doctor vanished. I could not see why marriage and medical school had become an either/or proposition. But for many women marriage was such a top priority that careers as well as love for Jesus had to be relegated to second place.

At the same time, some women stuck to their career goals, setting aside both human *and* spiritual relationships, and pursued top positions in business or academics. Love for Christ took a back seat to secular ambitions.

Nevertheless, I did find women, both at Wheaton College and later through Inter-Varsity Christian Fellowship at the University of Minnesota, who put Jesus Christ first in their lives. Because of this relationship, they prepared to serve Christ through their careers, either at home or abroad, without wavering from their purpose each time their hearts felt a flutter. For many of them marriage was postponed until they met husbands with similar goals and aspirations, so that as joint-heirs with Jesus Christ they could accomplish God's will for their lives. By waiting, these women chose marriage *and* mission instead of marriage *or* mission.

But such women were in the minority after World War 2, according to secular writers like Friedan and Christian analysts like Donald Dayton of Northern Baptist Theological Seminary. Dayton has helped me understand the climate I came from in China and why it stood in opposition to so much that I found in the United States after the war.

At every point in history the church is and has been caught in the tension between Christianity and culture. Jesus faced this problem as much as we do, for he was "tempted in every way, just as we are" (Heb 4:15). The example of Jesus challenges us not to conform to culture or go against it, but to transform culture.

During the days of the abolitionist movement and the revivals of the nineteenth century, lay persons—men and women—transcended their culture through their spontaneous participation in the life of the church. But as we shall see in more detail in chapter 9, such spontaneity was lost in the church after the war.

Writing about the mood of the evangelical church after World War 2, Dayton says:

As Evangelicals were more and more distanced from abolitionist controversies, they tended to fall back into biblical literalism. The forces of "fundamentalism" and "traditionalism" replaced the "evangelical spirit." Those groups that were produced by the spiritual movements and revivalism of the 19th century became more institutionalized. . . . And by and large there was a general accommodation to American culture. . . . In short, evangelical traditions became much more like those against which their foremothers and forefathers had protested.[3]

The suggestion that the church has accommodated herself to American culture is the saddest indictment of all.

## Changes in the '70s

When I last returned to the United States, it was 1974, not
1946. Instead of coming to North America for the first
time, by slow boat from China, I arrived for the seventh
time, by jet from the Philippines via Norway. Again I was
completely out of touch with the American heartbeat. It
was like history repeating itself. For fifteen years, as a missionary to the Philippines, I had been immersed in a culture where women, especially in the church, shared responsibilities with men. Since the church was not as professionalized as the American church, most of the one hundred
twenty congregations we had been in touch with were led
by lay people. Laywomen and laymen took turns preaching
and exercising spiritual gifts.

I had so submerged myself in this culture that I had forgotten my earlier struggles in the United States. During
the time in the Philippines, we had had three home leaves,
but the last two had been short summer furloughs divided
between Norway and the United States which did not give
us much time to take the American pulse.

In 1974 I found out that women's liberation—American
style—had happened during the years I had been absent.
The scanty reading I had done on the subject did not tell
me of the evangelical backlash against the movement. An
article in *Life* magazine had told about the Mormon backlash (*Fascinating Womanhood* by Helen Andelin)[4] and a secular backlash that advocated the "baby-doll-look,"illustrated on the cover of *Life* with pigtails and bright ribbons.

But it was only as I began to talk to individual women
that I started to comprehend the extent of the evangelical
backlash. I discovered that many Bible studies for women
no longer covered the great themes of salvation, faith, sanctification, eternal life and so on, but were preoccupied with
giving women proof texts for staying home, keeping house
and caring for their husbands and children.

"She gives me the feeling that she's on duty," a non-Christian woman complained to me about her Christian neighbor. "She can't even carry on a complete conversation —begins to feel guilty, and has to run back to the house." This woman went on to tell me about her divorce which had left her both wounded and apprehensive about the responsibility of raising a child alone. She was eager to discuss the claims of Christianity with anyone who had time to talk to her, but the Christian next door was on another wavelength.

After such conversations, I gradually began to realize that the evangelical woman was trapped between two wrong choices. She was obviously turned off by the radical feminism that defended lesbianism and abortion and that suggested pursuing a career regardless of the cost to the family. Rather than risk losing husband and children, it seemed safer to retreat to the kitchen to try to catch the flavor of the good old days. In the process, "Go into all the world and preach the gospel" was forgotten, along with "Worship the Lord your God and serve him only."

It was a heartbreaking discovery which was all the more disappointing since I had expected the reported renewal in the churches to have brought some changes. With all the claims about Joel's prophecy (2:28-29) being fulfilled, I had anticipated a new freedom among women to proclaim God's Word. But the renewal had not yet broken through the cultural barriers that had become a fad in the church. Women who stayed home as a reaction against women's liberation therefore neglected Christ's admonition to "go into all the world." But when we react against the world defensively, rather than move ahead offensively, the first thing that diminishes is our love for our Lord.

We forget so easily that Jesus promised that if we seek first his kingdom and his righteousness, all the rest shall be added to us (Mt 6:33). If our love relationship with him takes first priority, then all other relationships will find their rightful place in our hearts and schedules. The woman who focuses on Christ will therefore become a better wife and mother than the one who stays home all day out of a sense of duty, as a reaction or as a cop-out. To a woman who loves the Lord, the Word of God will burn as a fire in her bones, so that she must speak up for her Lord, whether the crowd be small or large, or whether the people be her own kin or those from a different culture (Jer 20:9).

When I presented such a challenge to a young church leader who had invited me to speak to the women of his church, he assured me, "But women have the freedom to do this right now."

"Then why aren't they doing it?" I asked.

"I guess they don't think they *can* do it," his answer came hesitantly. He was right on target.

**A Low Self-Image**
After we peel away the outer layers of sociological conditioning that keep women from a healthy relationship with Jesus Christ, we come to the problem of our own inner sense of unworthiness. That low self-image keeps many women acting like children, led by their husbands and fed by their pastors till they become like stuffed sheep. The obstacle of a low self-image keeps them from becoming anointed channels of God's love to people starved for friendship, in need of healing, desperately waiting to hear the Word of God for their predicament.

A couple of summers ago, I talked to a delightful woman who impressed me as having much to give to others. I asked her about her outreach. Did she have counseling opportunities? Was she sharing the good news in private or in public meetings?

She blushed and between stutters confessed, "My husband always tells me I should do more— that I have much to give—but you see, I have such a low self-image that it is hard for me to reach out to others. Of course, he tells me I shouldn't feel that way about myself."

As she talked, an old movie was replaying before my mind's eye. I had heard her husband speak a couple of years earlier. The sound of his voice came back to me with the words, "God's plan is for the husband to be the leader and the wife the follower. As we've been married all these years, I have become stronger in my leadership and my wife more willing to follow." Had the husband's strong views on male dominance unconsciously contributed to the wife's lack of self-worth? A low self-image doesn't just happen.

"My father always treated my mother as one of the kids," a good friend confided. Many women I have counseled have moved directly from a home where the father had the last word to a home where the husband played the same role. They first learned about their limitations as little girls growing up. Then as the men they married continued to treat them like children, the problem was compounded. Finally, if their churches do not encourage them to use their talents for others, they shrivel up in their service and often in their love for the Lord. Instead, they become encumbered, like Martha, in much serving (Lk 10:38-42). This often becomes a cover-up for their lack of courage to do anything that demands holy boldness.

Parents, husbands and pastors may contribute to this problem, or there may be an even deeper cause for a lack of self-worth.

## Fear
Hidden way down in our subconscious lurks an inner fear that feeds the low self-image even more persistently than the put-downs from without. John tells us that fear is the opposite of love in his famous passage, "There is no fear in love; but perfect love casts out fear: because fear hath tor-

ment. She that feareth is not made perfect in love" (1 Jn
4:18 KJV, my change).

For us as women part of discipleship means looking all
the fears in the face that spoil our relationship with Jesus
Christ. There is the slinking fear that if we appear a bit odd
or do not conform to cultural norms we might be ostra-
cized. I have been facing this fear in writing this book. The
approval of the evangelical community is a precious jewel
to me. Am I willing to give it up for the Pearl of great price?

Another woman finds herself nursing an unholy fear of
change which stems from a deeper fear of losing her security, her family and maybe even her femininity. Will she
become less appealing as a woman if her first concern centers on what is pleasing to her Savior?

But maybe the most prominent fear among sincerely
dedicated Christian women is the fear of going beyond
what God intends for them to do and say as women. This
fear will only be dispelled as it is held up to the mirror of
God's Word to discover if such a fear is well founded.

Paul tells us that "God did not give us a spirit of timidity,
but a spirit of power, of love and of self-discipline" (2 Tim
1:7). The very notion of worrying about whether I am
doing right or wrong suggests that I cannot trust God to
show me what is right. John says about such fear, "The
woman who fears is not made perfect in love" (1 Jn 4:18,
my changes).

Fear is the opposite of faith, which works through love.
Only faith can say, "I can trust the God of love to show me
one step of obedience at a time through his Word. I don't
need to know all the answers or even be able to give a full-
blown defense of what I'm doing."

The fears mentioned above cannot coexist with perfect
love, for perfect love casts out fear. God's kingdom is run
by love, not by fear. The Bible is full of invitations to God's
children to banish their fears and put their trust in a loving

God. Jesus predicts that before his return, there will come times of "men's hearts failing them for fear" (Lk 21:26 KJV). Maybe we are approaching these times.

But the woman who responds to God's love with all her heart and soul and mind will walk tall and straight as a daughter of the King. She will be released from the torment of low self-image and the fears that crippled her from sharing the good news. Instead, she will reach out in love to her neighbors—as a healing agent where people are hurting, as a catalyst for change where wrong needs to be righted, and as a prophetic voice where God's Word for the hour needs to be heard.

The holy boldness to reach out to others comes from a recognition of Jesus Christ as first love. His love grips our hearts as we first learn to worship the Lord our God. Significantly, it was to a woman that Jesus gave his most potent statement on worship: "God is a Spirit and his worshipers must worship in spirit and in truth." Her act of worship was acknowledging that Jesus was the Messiah. From that acknowledgment came her witness in the city of Samaria (Jn 4:1-42).

The women I admired who marched with us to prison in China after Pearl Harbor also acknowledged their faith in the great God of love. They led us boldly in singing:

O God our help in ages past,
Our hope for years to come,
Our shelter from the stormy blast,
And our eternal home!

Before the hills in order stood,
Or earth received her frame,
From everlasting Thou art God
To endless years the same.

Once more we need a theme song like that as women march into the unknown future, worshiping a loving God. Our worship will become a witness in a hurting world. What a great age to be a Christian woman!

*CHAPTER
THREE*

# Women Who
# Loved
# the Lord

**T**HE REASON I WAS SHOCKED
by the position of women in American society on my early
visits to this country was that I grew up with women who
were very different. I was extremely fortunate to have
been surrounded by models of Christian women who put
the Lord first in their lives.

**Mamma Torjesen**
One of my primary models was my own mother. As chil-
dren in China we would sing a little ditty as we waited for
our mother to return home:
  Mamma's coming soon
  Mamma's coming soon
  Mamma's coming soon
  I am glad.

The words were sung in our mother tongue, Norwegian: "Mamma kommer snart...Jeg er glad." My father had composed those lyrics as a message of hope for four kids who were missing their mamma very much.

Before I was born my mother and father had come from Norway to a distant outpost in northern China to bring the good news of God's love to the people who lived there. The church, school and clinic my parents started formed a triad expressing God's great love for the people of this forgotten region.

After years of winning the confidence of these beautiful Chinese people and sowing the seeds of the kingdom, marvelous results began to be seen. Women with bound feet who had never left their homes responded to God's love, learned to read and began traveling with my mother on gospel teams to nearby villages. They even went to a women's convention which was five days away by mule to meet other Christian women who had found a new identity. That's why four motherless children had to be content with Papa's makeshift "mothering" during Mamma's missionary journeys. I remember Papa struggling to find the clothes we should wear despite the fact that every drawer was left in perfect order by Mamma. And when we spilled milk on the table, he tried so hard to turn it into a joke.

Mothering did not come naturally to Papa. Now that I think about it, he may have looked on it as part of his sanctification process. But it was more than that. Mothering was part of his commitment to Jesus Christ. Long before Mamma and Papa were married they believed they were both called to be messengers of the good news. They also wanted children, and so agreed to take turns caring for them. Papa never went back on that promise; he had too much respect for Mamma and her identity as a servant of the living God.

Because my mother loved the Lord, she was concerned

with what was on God's heart—the salvation of the world. Her motive for missions was the same as that of the Moravians who cried, "May the Lamb who was slain receive the reward of his sufferings." For the sake of the Lamb who was slain my mother had to preach the gospel. Her identity as a woman was tied up in that life commitment. Whether as a wife, mother, hostess, preacher or nurse in a clinic ten days away from the nearest doctor, her roles always were integrated with her identity as a beloved disciple of Jesus.

## Madame Guyon

But my mother was not my only model. I was surrounded as a teen-ager by outstanding missionary women. In the China Inland Mission each man and woman had to spend two years in language school before marriage was permitted. Before family responsibilities crowded in on her, each woman had to have the Chinese language so well mastered that she could share the good news with a Chinese friend.

Some of these disciplined women, when we marched into prison camp with our few earthly possessions, carried with them the stories of women that were to greatly influence my life. Eager to learn about women who were committed to Jesus Christ, I spent months in prison poring over the diaries of Madame Guyon, Jessie Penn-Lewis and Catherine Booth.

I was especially interested in Madame Guyon because she also had been a prisoner. During her lifetime in France (1648-1717), she spent time in the Bastille and was banished to the city of Blois until her death. "Her sole crime was that of loving God," her biography states. "The ground of her offense was found in her supernatural devotion, and unmeasured attachment to Christ."[1]

Sometimes women today say that they are not good witnesses for Christ because of their lack of education. Maddame Guyon is a fitting model for such women. She was married at fifteen to a man twenty-two years her senior whose resident mother despised her devotion to Jesus Christ and her concern for the poor and sick. Against almost impossible odds she maintained her love for God.

As a young wife and mother in her early twenties, she explained her love for Christ with simplicity, "I loved Him without any motive or reason for loving." Was it because of his goodness, his mercy? She answered, "I well knew He was good and full of mercy. His perfections were my happiness. But I did not think of myself in loving Him. I loved Him and I burnt with love, because I loved Him. I loved Him in such a way that I could only love Him; but in loving Him I had no motive but Himself."[2]

After becoming a widow at twenty-eight, she wrote, "In losing all that is given, I found the Giver; . . . I found you in your very Self in the changeless—never to lose you again."[3]

During the years that followed, more and more priests, bishops and nuns came to sit at her feet to learn how to love God. She had a relationship like Priscilla and Apollos (Acts 18:24-28) with many young theologians, among them the archbishop of Cambrai—better known as Fenelon. But while the archbishop was her friend and disciple, King Louis XIV was her archenemy. Thomas Upham commented: "It is remarkable that a man whose mind was occupied with plans of vast extent, such as perhaps no French monarch before him had entertained, should enter into a contest, which may well be called a personal contest, with an unprotected woman. But it was."[4]

Madame Guyon did not speak publicly, yet through her writings and private conversations she influenced Catholics and Protestants in France, Germany, Holland, England and Switzerland. In our time, she is perhaps best known for her promotion of the hospice movement throughout Europe.

Madame Guyon's dedication is perhaps the best model of the kind of commitment Jesus called us to when he said:

If anyone wishes to be a follower of mine, she must leave self behind, she must take up her cross and come with me. Whoever cares for her own safety is lost, but if a woman will let herself be lost for my sake, she will find her true self. What will a woman gain by winning the whole world at the cost of her true self? (Mt 16:24-26 NEB, my changes)

Whenever stereotypes cloud our spiritual perception, we are in danger of resisting what the Holy Spirit is trying to say to us. If we allow the world to determine our identity, we are losing ourselves in the world, not in Christ. Paul might have had this freedom from roles in mind when he wrote, "So from now on we regard no one from a worldly point of view. . . . If anyone is in Christ, she is a new creation; the old has gone, the new has come!" (2 Cor 5:16-17, my changes).

Women are lost if they allow their roles to determine their identity. In prison I had models—living beside me and in the books I read—of women who put Christ first in their lives. Nevertheless, these models were not enough to keep me from forsaking Christ as my first love later on.

## My Own Early Mistakes

While I was in graduate school, I was happy to receive a sparkling diamond from Bob Malcolm, whom I had met through Inter-Varsity Christian Fellowship. We were sweethearts for several years at the University of Minnesota. Much prayer went into our courtship to be sure that God was leading us together. Our intention was to serve the Lord overseas as a missionary couple.

But neither of us was ready for marriage so we agreed to separate for two years when Bob started seminary. That year I accepted a teaching post at a secular institution that did not allow any Christian witness on campus. Evangelism had to be done by Christian teachers and students off campus. The challenge intrigued me. It seemed to fit God's perfect timing. My witness resulted in conversions to Christ. It had to be the Spirit working because I have never seen a situation since where so many students came on their own initiative to inquire about the Way. Those who were converted, quickly introduced their friends to Christ and thus the group grew through multiplication.

Because of the unique evangelistic opportunity and the shepherding needed among the young converts, I wrote to Bob when the two years were almost up about postponing our wedding for another year till he was through seminary. I was glad to find him willing to consider this plan. Also agreeing to my request to stay was my regional supervisor in the Christian organization I belonged to. His reaction was, "It would be immoral for you to leave."

Soon after this conversation, God further confirmed my desire to stay by miraculously providing a building across the street from campus to be used as a student center to expand the evangelistic work. I was hoping that either Bob would join me in this work after seminary or someone would replace me who had a similar evangelistic vision.

But others in the organization to which I belonged had less appreciation for a woman worker who wanted to postpone her wedding date for the sake of the ministry. My local supervisor thought it would be better for the organization that I leave on schedule and get married. After I had received word from headquarters that I had to leave, he and his wife moved into the student center as their home and base for their work and the local student work. The result was that the donor of the building felt he had been misled.

"I bought the house for you," he told me—not for me, but for the evangelistic outreach on the campus where I was teaching. (Some years later he required the building to be transferred to another group that majored in student evangelism on that campus.)

I have seldom felt as powerless as a woman as I did then in that organization run by men. In the power struggle between the regional and local supervisors, I was a voiceless woman. Furthermore those who should have given me spiritual guidance left me without it when I needed it most. The conflict was intensified because of my loyalty and devotion to this group to whom I had committed myself in the work of the gospel. For the sake of Christian unity, I could not leave the organization and continue teaching.

And so it was that with unresolved conflicts I married Bob Malcolm, the man I had loved for four years. We had the deep assurance that our union was in the will of God, though I was less sure about the timing. Bob adored me. He was as considerate and kind as he could be. But the timing problem colored our first four years together. Our early marriage was not marked by the usual conflicts of husband and wife trying to adjust to each other. But I had deep tensions within me as I worked out the heartbreak of having left my teaching post and the deep friendships with my students who had newly found Christ. At the same time, I was trying to accept a philosophy of Christian womanhood that came from people around me, not my husband. I thought I had to embrace a Christian version of the feminine mystique. Ironically, I was trying hard to accept the very ideas I had so violently rejected eight years earlier when I first arrived in the United States.

I had missed the call of God to walk straight ahead on the narrow path up the mountain, and I lost my way. I forgot Isaiah's words: "If you wander off the road to the right or the left, you will hear his voice behind you saying, 'Here is the road. Follow it' " (30:21 TEV). I was not listening.

Instead, I was beginning to listen to the common teaching that a woman's chief role is to be a support to her husband in his ministry, be a homemaker and raise children to follow the Lord. I failed to test this teaching with Scripture as the Bereans had done ("They received the message with great eagerness and examined the Scriptures every day to see if what Paul said was true" Acts 17:11).

I was a woman at war with myself. While I tried to agree with my conscious mind to a view that limited a woman's contribution to the kingdom, my subconscious revolted within me. I knew I was being untrue to myself, my parents, and everything they had taught me about Christian womanhood. The results were disastrous. None of us can ignore the truths taught us from the Bible by godly parents and remain unscathed. Overcome with grief over the ministry I had left and trying to fit into the role of a submissive homemaker, I felt myself losing my identity. Who was I? For the first time in my life, I developed the "I'm just a woman" syndrome.

When I could no longer look on myself as a precious disciple and disciplemaker, a friend of Jesus Christ, I became sick. Many months were spent in bed with an undiagnosed fever. After the fever subsided, I went into a deep depression. Guilt feelings about having left my first love swept over me—some from God and some based on false regret.

The example of my mother, who started a new missionary career in Taiwan after she was sixty, only added to my sense of guilt. My mother thought I should be out of the house, evangelizing the world and using all my God-given gifts to help others. As a nurse and a Christian, she believed very strongly that if we are not doing what God intends us to be doing, we will get sick. She often identified women in her own age bracket who were sick because they were not obedient to the revealed will of God. She did not believe that every person had to be a missionary or that everyone had the same gifts, but she believed that every person who was a disciple of Jesus Christ had gifts to be offered back to Jesus for the building of the kingdom.

God's plan for the world involves having people utilize the talents he has given them. In *The Truth about You,* the authors write:

> Can you begin to imagine how the world would benefit if people were educated and employed on the basis that each person is gifted? Regardless of how old or young you are—how low on the totem pole you see yourself— how impoverished your education or upbringing— you have been given good gifts. You have been designed and have a role to play that will fulfill you and please others. Discover your design![5]

My mother would have said "Amen." During my identity crisis, she saw me go against that design. She had seen me leave my teaching post where I was deeply involved in evangelism. And now I was so entrenched in the mystique that I thought I had to focus on housekeeping. Nevertheless, my mother recognized that my crisis could not be blamed on Bob. And she was still so eager to see her grandchild that —with her usual flair—she managed to arrive from Taiwan on the very day I had my first baby.

We had some very happy times together as well as some tense moments. She was hurt to see me conform to what she called male veneration and the emphasis on keeping women in the background. As I defended this foreign doctrine, she just shook her grey head and looked at me with sad blue eyes. I knew she bled for me.

Years before, Mother had written in the Bible she gave me for my twenty-first birthday, "My daughter, keep thy father's commandment, and forsake not the law of thy mother" (Prov 6:20 KJV). All through my childhood, my parents had taught me that in Christ there is no difference between male and female (Gal 3:28). Whenever we discussed the inequality between men and women in pre-Mao

China, they attributed this to pagan values. I did not know until I came to the United States how much these same pagan values from Europe, instead of Asia, had penetrated the church.

### Receiving a Christ Identity
After having adapted to the cultural environment of the United States, years passed before I realized how much I had been looking for my identity in the popular roles I played. Very gradually I started to discover that the Bible is filled with stories of women whose roles flowed from their identity as Jesus' beloved disciples.

When I thought of disciples following Jesus, I had always thought of men like Peter, James and John leaving their nets. But then I discovered another part of the story. In Luke 8:1-3, I read about Joanna, Susanna, Mary Magdalene and many other women who left their roles as daughters and wives to follow Jesus and spread the good news. I was fascinated by the fact that Mary Magdelene announced the resurrection to Jesus' disciples. Earlier, Jesus had accepted her as a person, giving her a new identity as a disciple. In doing so, Jesus may have been building on the foundation of her outgoing personality. This stood her in good stead when she encountered rejection from the disciples who would not believe her message. For Jesus, Mary Magdalene's identity as a loyal disciple made possible her role as a proclaimer of the good news.

Gradually I began to see that Jesus was more interested in a woman's obedience than in her roles. In the Mary and Martha story (Lk 10:38-42), Martha was complaining because her sister had neglected her traditional role of preparing the food for guests. She went instead and listened at Jesus' feet. Mary, it seems, took the position of a disciple who wanted to be identified with a great teacher, just as Paul had spoken of himself as one who had been "brought up . . . at the feet of Gamaliel" (Acts 22:3 KJV).

Many have interpreted this story to mean that there are
two options open to women: the role of the scholar or the
role of the busy hostess. But Jesus did not give Mary and
Martha that kind of a choice. He rebuked Martha for her
busy-work and said, "Only one thing is needed. Mary has
chosen what is better, and it will not be taken away from
her" (Lk 10:42). Mary's identity as a disciple was more important to Jesus than her role as a hostess, regardless of how
much work was left to be done in the kitchen. Jesus also
desired that Martha put her identity as a disciple ahead of
her social responsibilities.

Another passage that had never made sense to me before
was the story of the woman who told Jesus, "Blessed is the
mother who gave you birth and nursed you" (Lk 11:27).
Jesus did not refuse her compliment, but used the occasion
to challenge the woman to a deeper faith. While he was
grateful to his mother for her procreative role, Jesus suggested that there was a greater dimension to the lives of
women. "Blessed rather are those who hear the word of
God and obey it" (v. 28), says Jesus, thinking of Mary who
conceived him in cooperation with the Holy Spirit. Her
obedience started with her declaration of her identity as
the "handmaid of the Lord" (Lk 1:38 KJV). Jesus was thus
inviting all women to find their identity in relationship to
their God.

As I have struggled over my own identity, I have often
found comfort in the promise of Jesus that "whoever does
God's will is my brother and sister and mother" (Mk 3:35).
The context here is that Jesus was told that his mother and
brothers were waiting to see him outside a crowded house.
He responded to the news by asking the question, "Who
is my mother and my brothers?" Jesus answered by suggesting that any man or woman who wants to be identified
with him as an obedient disciple will be given the honor

of being called his brother, sister or mother.

As Jesus' answer has been music to my own ears, how much more to the ears of women of that day who had no identity other than motherhood? Among the New Testament women who found an identity in their relationship to Jesus Christ as a disciple, we find mothers like Lois and her daughter Eunice who brought up Timothy in the knowledge of the Scriptures (2 Tim 1:5; 3:14-15).

Innumerable women through the ages have found their identity as disciples of Jesus Christ and then let their roles flow from that identity. I mourn that for many years I missed this message and departed from the teaching of my godly parents. Why did I lose my way? Because to walk the road with Jesus against the tide of popular teaching means keeping to a very narrow road. "Few there be that find it," Jesus predicted.

Today there are not enough women who burn with a desire to sit at Jesus' feet in the tradition of Mary.

**From Pain to Promise**
Looking back to my own years of playing the Martha role, I have often asked why I was not spared this experience. The answer has come back over and over again: "You would never have understood women who are controlled by the traditions of men unless you had gone through it yourself." God "comforts us in all our troubles, so that we can comfort those in any trouble with the comfort we ourselves have received from God" (2 Cor 1:4).

In retrospect, I can view this whole experience, which started with leaving my teaching post, as one of those difficult situations that God turns upside-down for our good, just as he did with my years in prison camp. I can look back with the deep assurance that "in all things God works for the good of those who love him" (Rom 8:28). If I should ever decide to have one verse tattooed all over my body, it would have to be Romans 8:28!

Through this experience I have also learned something about forgiveness and the joy in heaven over a sinner who repents (Lk 15:7). I have been that sinner. And like the sinful woman in Luke, I know that the one who needs much forgiveness loves much (Lk 7:47).

As a forgiven sinner, I have discovered that the same God who pardons also heals our emotional illnesses and the bad memories from our past. Therefore, I can look back on all the difficult situations of my life and join with the psalmist in the great burst of worship and praise:

"Bless the LORD, O my soul;
and all that is within me,
bless his holy name!
Bless the LORD, O my soul,
and forget not all his benefits,
who forgives all your iniquity,
who heals all your diseases." (Ps 103:1-3 RSV)

Through the process of forgiveness and healing, I began again to worship, finding my identity in a first-love relationship with Jesus Christ. What a long way I had to travel before my marriage could begin to reflect the relationship my mother and father had to the Lord and to each other, based on the belief that they were both called to offer their bodies "as living sacrifices, holy and pleasing to God—which is . . . spiritual worship" (Rom 12:1).

# PART TWO

# The
# Explosive
# Gospel

# CHAPTER FOUR

# The Walls Come Tumbling Down

THE MARBLE STAIRCASE I had been admiring suddenly became a place of anguish. Stunned, I stood still, watching Patricia as she continued her sprightly flight down the steps. The sting of discrimination pierced deep inside me.

Patricia and I had just been released from three years in a Japanese prison camp in China. Along with sixteen hundred others, we had suffered together and recognized each other as fellow prisoners. Then came V-J Day! American paratroopers dropped straight out of the heavens to release us. Rejoicing together in our new freedom, we all left the familiar camp with its electrified barbed wire and wide moat. Our first stop had been this beautiful hotel in Tsingtao, which the Japanese had preserved amazingly well through the war years.

Awed by all the grandeur, I bubbled, "Isn't this exciting to be in a place like this?"

Patricia shot her answer back at me as she skipped on: "Oh, I've always lived in places like this. This is nothing new to me." Patricia wanted to remind me that, before concentration camp, she came from a wealthy businessman's family, while I was just a poor missionary kid!

I have observed the same drama enacted during and after college for many young people. Like prison camp, the campus becomes a melting pot for men and women, rich and poor, and representatives from a variety of racial groups. Many choose their life partners in this cosmopolitan atmosphere. Some also discover or strengthen their relationship with Jesus Christ during the college years. Deep friendships often grow out of small-group sharing sessions where students meet to explore their faith. In such a Christian community, the barriers of race, class and sex are often forgotten.

But after college, the walls of separation are inevitably re-erected in the minds of the new graduates. Why? Because the barriers are still there in everyone's mind, and we forget to resist the pressure to conform. Soon the new graduate discovers that the way up the economic and social ladder means knowing the right people. Hence, there isn't time to get involved with the losers in society—the cheaters, prostitutes and drunkards with whom Jesus mingled so freely. Slowly the former Christian radicals find themselves living just as they condemned their parents for living. Like Patricia, they are back in the same ruts.

Those who get married, having been former campus sweethearts, also face existing barriers when they move into the real world. Again they slip into the patterns they despised from the perspective of campus life. But there it was easier. There they were part of a Christian support group. And there they sat next to each other in philosophy class, competing for the same coveted grade-point average. But now the successful young male leaves for the office in his new three-piece suit to do big things out in the world, while his wife stays home, snowed under by dishes and diapers, to face the next ten hours alone in a crowded apartment with lively toddlers.

## Jesus' Example

Against the background of a world of inequities, the gospel comes to us with hope. The God who refuses to give us mass-produced, legalistic answers to our questions also refuses to divide us into groups of more fortunate and less fortunate human beings. Jesus never sanctioned prejudice based on sex, class or race. He dared to break all three barriers when he sat down by the well outside Sychar and started talking to a woman—something a Jewish man was not supposed to do. But she was not just a woman; she was a woman of questionable reputation, from a lower class, who espoused a heretical religion! No wonder the disciples were agog when they arrived "and were surprised to find him talking with a woman" (Jn 4:27).

But Jesus was not uncomfortable. Nor was he hungry when they offered him lunch. He explained his great sense of fulfillment by telling them indirectly what had happened with the woman. She had found her first love that day as Jesus offered her living water. The water was so satisfying that she immediately rushed to tell the rest of the town about it. Some day the disciples would reap where this woman had sown, for in Acts 8:4-25 we read about a strong church in Samaria. But Jesus reminded them, "I sent you to reap what you have not worked for. Others have done the hard work, and you have reaped the benefits of their labor" (Jn 4:38). Could it be that Jesus was giving this woman credit for a part in the evangelization of Samaria?

In these revolutionary words, Jesus cut any ties his followers thought he had with the Jewish, male-dominated, upper-class religious hierarchy. That group felt the sting of his words when he said,

> They love the place of honor at banquets and the most important seats in the synagogues; they love to be greeted in the marketplaces and to have men call them "Rabbi."

> But you are not to be called "Rabbi," for *you have only one Master and you are all brothers.* And do not call anyone on earth "father," for you have one Father, and he is in heaven. Nor are you to be called "teacher" for you have one Teacher, the Christ. *The greatest among you will be your servant.* (Mt 23:6-11, my emphasis)

Somehow we have forgotten these words as we have replaced the Jewish male religious hierarchy with the usually all-white, male-dominated, well-salaried religious hierarchies of most churches. Everything Jesus taught and did during his earthly pilgrimage stands in sharp contrast to this aspect of our visible Christianity. Words like hierarchy, authority, control, dominance and lordship, or chain-of-command are difficult to find in his teaching.

When James and John asked Jesus for privileged seats in heaven —one on his right and the other on his left—Jesus said, "You do not know what you are asking." Had they missed the whole point of his teaching? He continued later, "You know that those who are regarded as rulers of the Gentiles lord it over them, and their high officials exercise authority over them. Not so with you. Instead, whoever wants to become great among you must be your servant, and whoever wants to be first must be slave of all. For even the Son of Man did not come to be served, but to serve, and to give his life as a ransom for many" (Mk 10:38, 42-45).

Jesus' call to servanthood is perhaps the hardest call he has given us. Through this call, he asks us to overcome all barriers of discrimination and choose a life of service, rather than leadership, authority or dominance. Such a teaching is directly contrary to our human striving for one-upmanship.

We build the hierarchies of authority that separate us while Jesus has called us to unity through loving service. We confuse human structures with "divine order." Because we are human, we need appointed tasks and division of labor in home, church and society. But confusion sets in when we use our appointed human position to lord it over another in the name of "spiritual authority" or "divine order." When shepherds and husbands come between Christ and the individual believer, they ignore a basic pillar of truth: "For there is one God, and one mediator between God and men [and women], the man Christ Jesus" (1 Tim 2:5 KJV).

It is as a mediator between God and humanity that Jesus calls us to join the new order of servants. The call is wrapped in an invitation to enter a relationship with Jesus Christ: "If you love me, you will do what I command.... You are my friends if you do what I command" (Jn 14:15; 15:14). These invitations to a relationship show that his authority is based on people's *love* for him. He never demanded that anyone obey him because he was the Messiah or the Shepherd.

Jesus taught by example. At the Last Supper, he wanted to give the disciples their final review of "Servanthood 101," so he "got up from the meal, took off his outer clothing, and wrapped a towel around his waist. After that, he poured water into a basin and began to wash his disciples' feet, drying them with the towel that was wrapped around him" (Jn 13:4-5).

He chose to do the chore that wives in that culture performed for their husbands, and slaves for their masters, thus breaking both the barriers. He goes on: "Now that I, your Lord and Teacher, have washed your feet, you also should wash one another's feet.... Now that you know these things, you will be blessed if you do them" (13:14, 17).

Why are we so preoccupied with stratifications in home, church and society when Jesus calls us to an attitude of loving servanthood? He is inviting us to a new order where we are all brothers and sisters of equal rank, eager to serve one another, regardless of race, class or sex. This attitude of servanthood is only possible because, as we come to the cross as sinners, we are all at the same level.

Jesus did not use famous religious leaders, philanthropic businessmen or patriarchal fathers as examples of faith. Instead he chose a child!

He called a little child and had him stand among them. And he said: "I tell you the truth, unless you change and become like little children, you will never enter the kingdom of heaven. Therefore, whoever humbles himself like this child is the greatest in the kingdom of heaven. And whoever welcomes a little child like this in my name welcomes me." (Mt 18:2-5)

Jesus' words were particularly significant because in his day "children had no rights; and girls and the offspring of slaves particularly were held in low esteem." Hans-Ruedi Weber goes on to describe the lot of the boys: "Those who could not yet recite the *Shema,* the basic affirmation of the Jewish faith, and those who had not yet memorized the precepts of the *Torah,* the will of the living God, could not fully participate in the worship and life of the covenant people. Jesus' way with children was in sharp contrast to what was current in his own world. So astonishing were his words and gestures that even his disciples could not comprehend them."[1]

History is dotted with "little people"—helpless children and the oppressed—who are miles ahead of the average, religious, middle-class adult in their grasp of the kingdom. And yet we continue to ignore this aspect of Jesus' teaching and erect walls that divide whites from nonwhites, young from old, rich from poor, men from women, and the old established residents from the aliens who have arrived "late" on the scene.

Jesus is very patient with all of us and keeps the invitation open: "Take my yoke upon you and learn from me, for I am gentle and humble in heart, and you will find rest for your souls. For my yoke is easy and my burden is light" (Mt 11:29-30). Jesus is the only leader in history who can rightfully claim to be humble and gentle. He calls us to follow in his steps. While we think of a leader as a person of power and authority, Jesus emerges as a helpless infant from the hiddenness of a stable. This is the paradox of the gospel. Jesus never outgrew his humble beginnings. He never became a political leader in the court of the oppressors, like Joseph, Moses and Daniel. He remained the carpenter's son and called people to a childlike faith and a humble servant attitude.

## The Early Church

The church that was founded by the apostles was nourished by reminders to follow in the footsteps of Jesus. In every age bands of believers have lived out dangerously the dictates of their Master. But perhaps life in the early church period sounds most exciting to us. Those despised disciples had the advantage of starting out right, on the day of Pentecost.

About eight hundred years before that day, the prophet Joel had looked through God's telescope and seen what would happen that day. Living at a time when women were owned like cattle, and slaves were used as beasts of burden, Joel wrote what God revealed to him: "The day shall come when I will pour out my spirit on all mankind; your sons and your daughters shall prophesy, . . . I will pour out my spirit in those days even upon slaves and slave-girls" (2:28-29 NEB).

Long before Paul wrote about Jews and Greeks being one

in Christ, Joel visualized a day without racial, sexual or economic tension. God would not just pour his spirit on the Jews, but on all nations. The result of this outpouring of God's Spirit would be daughters joining sons in proclaiming God's message and thus erasing the power struggle between the sexes. Among the men and women who would receive God's Spirit would be the despised slaves. Finally, class differences would disappear. What a beautiful vision for Joel to share with his and future generations. The impossible would become a reality because of the gospel.

Perhaps Joel was leaning over the banisters of heaven the day his prophecy was fulfilled. It was the day of Pentecost, the day when the church was born. Men and women had been waiting for this day (Acts 1:12-14). As "all of them were filled with the Holy Spirit and began to speak in other tongues" (Acts 2:4), Peter rose to his feet and announced that this day Joel's prophecy was being fulfilled. Then he quoted the exact text (Acts 2:16-18).

As we read the story in Acts 2 we get the feeling of great joy and creative power being released on the large crowd. What an exciting day! We can imagine the awe as those first church members found themselves all leveled in the presence of God. For all who were oppressed the gates of bronze were broken that day, the bars of iron were cut asunder, and the mountains of prejudice were leveled (Is 45:2). Slaves were assured of belonging to the family of God. Their new identity established within that family, the slaves in the early church were equipped by the Holy Spirit to bring the good news to their pagan households.

In his excellent work *Evangelism in the Early Church,* Michael Green describes recent archaeological findings that add color to the historical records of "the general infiltration of the middle and upper classes of Roman society by Christianity through the lives and words of slaves and freedmen in their employment."[2] It is difficult for us to grasp the full significance of this without reminding our-selves of the status of slaves in Roman society. Aristotle said that "a slave is a living tool, just as a tool is an inanimate slave," and Cato advised people to "sell worn out oxen, blemished cattle ... old tools, an old slave, a sickly slave, whatever else is useless."[3]

Against this backdrop, Christians adopted loving con-cern for slaves as brothers and sisters. According to Igna-tius, such love led to the use of church funds to buy free-dom for a number of slaves.[4]

Along with the slaves, the women of the early church found liberation as they shared in the agape feasts, in wor-ship, in Holy Communion and in the proclamation of the gospel to a pagan world. Michael Green describes women who "gossiped Christianity at the laundry," and he suggests that "these same women were among the most successful evangelists. Whether we look as early as 1 Peter or as late as the *Apostolic Constitutions,* the words and example of the Christian wife are taken for granted as the major influence through which the husband's conversion is looked for."[5] The prominence of women in evangelism, semiprivate and public, continued into the second century. Women prophe-sied, preached and faced martyrdom along with their brothers in the faith. In the cases of slaves and women, the structure of society was not changed, but the attitude within the church family was changed.

People today who do not understand the law of love ask why Paul didn't speak out against the structures that divid-ed men from women, rich from poor, Jews from Greeks. Paul answers the question in his letter to Corinth: "Though I am free and belong to no man, I make myself a slave to everyone, to win as many as possible. To the Jews I became like a Jew, to win the Jews. . . . To those not having the law I became like one not having the law . . . so as to win those not having the law. To the weak I became weak, to win the weak. I have become all things to all men so that by all possible means I might save some. I do all this for the sake of the gospel, that I may share in its blessing" (1 Cor 9:19-23).

For the sake of the gospel Paul had to make many concessions which may look like inconsistencies. But as a follower of Jesus Christ, he was not doubleminded when he acted like a Jew one day and a Gentile the next. His great passion was to introduce men and women, rich and poor, Jew and Gentile, to Jesus Christ.

Virginia Mollenkott defends such a position by saying, "For the first-century apostles, the major mission was to spread the gospel. There were many things about the culture that were antichristian, including slavery and the male domination of women. But first things first. Although the New Testament clearly contains the principles which, when obeyed, would do away with slavery, racism, and male supremacy, it was important not to detract from the basic message of Jesus as Savior by trying to correct all social injustices overnight."[6]

In the nineteenth century, David Sherman had the same idea as he wrote "Woman's Place in the Gospel." He explained that "while yielding for a time to the form of the institution [of slavery], the apostles laid down principles which cut away the foundations of the system.... [The] same method was adopted in the case of woman.... The apostles began the elevation and education of woman, and left the movement to flow on so far and in such channels as Providence and the current of events might open for it, thus preparing the way for a much broader and grander work than they themselves were permitted to perform."[7]

### A God of Justice
As men and women, blacks and whites, rich and poor gather together to worship the Lord Jesus Christ, they will discover that the love that will flow between them will change

all oppressive situations and remove the sting of discrimi-
nations. Only then will the schisms in the body of Christ
be healed, for "you are the body of Christ, and each one of
you is a part of it. . . . There should be no division in the
body, but that its parts should have equal concern for each
other" (1 Cor 12:27, 25).

Our God is a God of justice. This theme was picked up by
Mary when she realized God had chosen her—an unknown
woman, from the despised Jewish nation, from a family too
poor to rent a hotel room—for a great mission. Mary's burst
of praise continues to be heard in churches around the
world:

> My soul magnifies the Lord,
> and my spirit rejoices in God my Savior,
> for he has regarded the low estate of his handmaiden.
> For behold, henceforth all generations will call me
>     blessed;
> for he who is mighty has done great things for me,
> and holy is his name. . . .
>
> He has shown strength with his arm,
> he has scattered the proud in the imagination of their
>     hearts,
> he has put down the mighty from their thrones,
> and exalted those of low degree;
> he has filled the hungry with good things,
> and the rich he has sent empty away.
> He has helped his servant Israel,
> in remembrance of his mercy" (Lk 1:46-49, 51-54 RSV).

Mary, the poor peasant woman from a colonized nation,
had heard the call to cooperate with God in the redemption
of the world. Even before she gave birth to the Savior, she
announced that the three barriers of oppression had been

broken. I can hear Mary's voice across the centuries telling us that though the world is still full of injustice, that is not the way God wants it to be.

Perhaps the highest form of expression of our love for God comes at those moments when we feel most intensely the oppressive situations around us. We have only one place to turn for perfect justice:

I will sing of your love and justice;

to you, O LORD, I will sing praise. (Ps 101:1)

# CHAPTER FIVE

# Women in Jesus' Day

T HE SUNDAY MORNING service presented a dilemma. "Pastor Malcolm, I hope you can understand this. We cannot let you preach in the morning service. But do you mind if we ask your wife to speak?" After clearing his throat, the pastor continued in his Norwegian "brogue": "You see, you can't speak Norwegian, and for the sake of the newcomers from Norway, we have a rule in our church that only Norwegian be spoken in the morning service. But in the evening service, we allow a little bit of English, so you may preach then," he added with obvious relief.

We were sitting in the pastor's study of the Norwegian Evangelical Free Church in Brooklyn, the local church I had joined on my arrival in the United States. Now as furloughed missionaries from the Philippines, we were planning meetings to be divided between the English and Norwegian departments of this church. And we were facing a language crisis. Since two departments with two separate services going on under one roof had been initiated to resolve the language problem, the Norwegian immigrants were eager to keep the Norwegian services pure—with only the language of heaven!

As all of this background came alive in the pastor's study, we found ourselves enjoying a modern version of the "Jew and Greek, male and female" dilemma.

Even though Bob was the ordained minister, I could speak Norwegian. I was the Hebrew of Hebrews, and my husband was the Greek. The pastor was forced to choose between a female Jew or a male Greek. Culturally, it would have been more acceptable to assign a woman to speak in the evening service. But why should the gender of the speaker proclaiming God's Word make a difference?

**A Golden Age for Women**
Let us look at how Jesus treated the women who were among his friends and those who assisted him in the spread of the good news. It began with his mother, Mary, who identified herself as the handmaid of the Lord. When Mary received the announcement of her coming pregnancy, she trusted God to handle her relationship with Joseph. Mary did not panic with fear that she might be rejected by the man to whom she was betrothed or stoned for such an unorthodox pregnancy.[1] Her heart was open to God as she exclaimed: "Behold the handmaid of the Lord; be it unto me according to thy word." She had her priorities straight: first, as the handmaid of the Lord, and second, as Joseph's wife-to-be. Her first love was God himself. Her trust was in him, and he in turn trusted her to bear the Christ-child.

Every woman since Mary who has found a love relationship with God has been given the commission to bring

Christ to her generation. That's why the women who loved Jesus followed him along with the male disciples:

Jesus traveled about from one town and village to another, proclaiming the good news of the kingdom of God. The Twelve were with him, and also some women who had been cured of evil spirits and diseases: Mary (called Magdalene) from whom seven demons had come out; and Joanna the wife of Cuza, the manager of Herod's household; Susanna; and many others. These women were helping to support them out of their own means. (Lk 8:1-3)

Walking between towns with Jesus these women must have carefully listened to all the instructions he was giving to those who were part of his traveling seminary. Perhaps the Twelve were not aware how eagerly the women grasped the truths taught. But the angels must have taken note of their attentiveness, for at the empty tomb an angel reminded the women: " 'Remember how he told you, while he was still with you in Galilee: The Son of Man must be delivered into the hands of sinful men, be crucified and the third day be raised again.' Then they remembered his words" (Lk 24: 6-7).

Yes, the women remembered their training. And they were ready for their big assignment: to tell the Twelve and the world the greatest news of all history, that Jesus Christ had risen from the dead (Lk 24:9-11). Many have wondered why God chose to let women bring the news of Christ's resurrection to the male disciples. Wasn't this his creative way of ushering in the new order on that glorious resurrection morning?

Women were among the last to remain at Jesus' cross and were the first to his empty tomb. It was apparently to Mary Magdalene that Jesus spoke first after his resurrection, telling her to proclaim his news to his brothers (Jn 20: 17-18). Mary Magdalene and the other women were also among the disciples who waited for the Holy Spirit in the upper room. In fact, all through the Gospels and the book of Acts women are mentioned among the inner circle of followers of Christ.

## Paul's Journeys

After Pentecost God chose a stubborn, brilliant Jew to be the chief architect of the church. Paul was "circumcised on the eighth day, of the people of Israel, of the tribe of Benjamin, a Hebrew of Hebrews; in regard to the law, a Pharisee . . . as for legalistic righteousness, faultless." Yet Paul was quick to add, "but whatever was to my profit I now consider loss for the sake of Christ. . . . I consider them rubbish, that I may gain Christ" (Phil 3:5-8).

In the light of his primary relationship with Christ, Paul's Jewishness, his maleness, his status in society as a Pharisee meant absolutely nothing. The man who had thanked God daily, as all God-fearing Jewish males did, that he was not a Gentile, not a slave and not a woman, now wrote the revolutionary statement: "There is neither Jew nor Greek, slave nor free, male nor female, for you are all one in Christ Jesus" (Gal 3:28). Because of his love for Jesus, he loved the slave, Onesimus, and because the love of Christ constrained him, he could write with deep affection to all the gentile churches he had founded. The same love led him to mention women among his coworkers in almost every city and seaport he touched.

Paul was first introduced to women in the church while he was yet a persecutor of it. Knowing that women had proclaimed the Word of God on the day of Pentecost and that "more and more men *and women* believed in the Lord" (Acts 5:14), it was natural that, as he went from "house to house, he dragged off men *and women* and put them in prison" (Acts 8:3, my emphasis).

Another surprise for Paul was to find women among his

persecutors after his conversion. When Paul first preached to Jews and Gentiles in Antioch, "the Jews incited the God-fearing women of high standing and the leading men of the city. They stirred up persecution against Paul and Barnabas, and expelled them from their region" (Acts 13: 50). The preaching of the gospel led to decision—either for or against Christ—among both men and women.

After the call to Macedonia (Acts 16:9-10), Paul crossed the waters to Europe, hoping to find the man from Macedonia he had seen in his vision. Instead, God led Paul to a group of women praying on the banks of the Gangites River where Paul discovered Lydia, who would become a leader of the first church founded on the European continent. "The Lord opened her heart to respond to Paul's message. When she and the members of her household were baptized, she invited us to her home," writes Luke, the author of Acts (16:14-15). After a stint in prison, Paul and Silas again stayed at Lydia's house and encouraged the new Christians there (Acts 16:40).

In his letter to the church that started in Lydia's home, Paul writes years later, "I thank my God upon every remembrance of you, ... for your fellowship in the gospel from the first day until now" (Phil 1:3, 5 KJV). He also has an interesting message for two women in the church: "I plead with Euodia and I plead with Syntyche to agree with each other in the Lord ... these women who have contended at my side in the cause of the gospel" (Phil 4:2-3). Many have speculated about the cause of these women's quarrel. Had they argued about whether to serve cake or cookies for a church reception? Paul obviously does not trivialize the argument between these women who had labored by his side. Probably Chrysostom, a father of the church in the fourth century, is much closer to the truth when he suggests that their differences had something to do with their spiritual nurturing of the congregations that met in their homes.[2]

Paul also encountered women among the earliest disciples in Thessalonica. Luke writes, "Some of the Jews were persuaded and joined Paul and Silas, as did a large number of God-fearing Greeks and not a few prominent women" (Acts 17:4). Then he went on to Berea where we read that "they received the message with great eagerness and examined the Scriptures every day to see if what Paul said was true. Many of the Jews believed, as did also a number of prominent Greek women and many Greek men" (Acts 17: 11-12). They were commended by Luke for questioning Paul's teaching and checking it out with Scripture on a daily basis.

From Berea Paul went to Athens where he preached on Mars Hill. Very few converts are mentioned in this ancient city. Luke reports on those who believed: "Among them was Dionysius, a member of the Areopagus, also a woman named Damaris, and a number of others" (Acts 17:34). Why was Damaris mentioned? Did she start a church in her home? We can only speculate.

Paul's next stop was Corinth where he lodged in the home of Priscilla and Aquila. We read in 1 Corinthians 16:19 that a church met in their home. Paul mentions them again in Romans 16:3-5: "Greet Priscilla and Aquila, my fellow workers in Christ Jesus. They risked their lives for me. Not only I but all the churches of the Gentiles are grateful to them."

At Cenchreae, a port of Corinth on the Saronic Gulf, Paul found another outstanding woman: "I commend to you our sister Phoebe, who is a minister of the church at Cenchreae. . . . Assist her in any matter in which she may have need of you. For she herself has been made an overseer to many people, including myself" (Rom 16:1-2 Montgomery).[3] Chrysostom says of Phoebe and Priscilla: "These were noble women, hindered in no way by their sex . . . and this is as might be expected, for in Christ

Jesus there is neither male nor female."[4]

Space does not permit us to mention all the women who were associated with Paul in his journeys, such as the four prophesying daughters of Philip (Acts 21:8-9) and all the women "who labored much in the Lord" and are named at the close of Paul's letters. There may have even been a female apostle.

*Junian* is referred to in Romans 16:7: "Greet Andronicus and Junias, my relatives who have been in prison with me. They are outstanding among the apostles, and they were in Christ before I was." In the Greek, the name is *Junian,* which is the accusative form for either the feminine, Junia, or the masculine, Junias. Although most modern translations assume it is masculine, *The Interpreter's Dictionary* recognizes there is some doubt: "Grammatically it might be feminine, though this seems less probable, partly because the person referred to is an apostle."

Chrysostom, on the other hand, assumed that *Junian* referred to a woman. And because of his proximity to her in time, his assumption must be considered. "Oh! how great is the devotion of this woman, that she should be even counted worthy the appellation of apostle."[5] Chrysostom's praise becomes even more believable when we see how unlikely it would be for him to refer to a woman as an apostle if he were not convinced she deserved that title, for he also wrote: "Among the wild beasts, there is none more harmful than woman."[6]

Thus, from the very first, women were active in the cause of Christ. Michael Green points out in *Evangelism in the Early Church:*

> The New Testament tells us of women labouring in evangelism, acting as hostess to the Church in their houses, prophesying and speaking in tongues, and acting as deaconesses. This prominence of women continued ... in the second century. Sometimes it would

be exercised through public speaking, sometimes through martyrdom. The preaching of a Maximilla, a Thecla, or the four daughters of Philip the evangelist had a power which was not to be denied.[7]
Yet this seems inconsistent with some of Paul's statements. Did women proclaim the good news? Or were they silent?

## Is Silence Golden?

In 1 Corinthians 11:5 Paul says that women who pray and prophesy in public should cover their heads. This was the cultural standard of Paul's day for married women. Prophesying here does not mean foretelling the future, as the Old Testament prophets sometimes did. In 1 Corinthians 14:3 Paul says, "Everyone who prophesies speaks to men for their strengthening, encouragement and comfort."

The significance of these statements is that it is implicit in them that *women were praying and prophesying in public.* They apparently did this in the public worship services of the early church. We get a little more detail of how these meetings were conducted in 1 Corinthians 14:26: "When you come together, everyone has a hymn, or a word of instruction, a revelation, a tongue or an interpretation. All of these must be done for the strengthening of the church." Paul then goes on to suggest in the next few verses (29-33) that two or three prophets can speak in the same meeting. If God gives a message to a person who is seated, the person speaking must be willing to give that person the floor, "for you can all prophesy in turn so that everyone may be instructed and encouraged" (v. 31).

It would be wonderful if once again our worship services were marked by lay persons prophesying one by one as Paul suggests in 1 Corinthians 14:26-33 and 36-40. But right in the middle of these beautiful instructions come the verses on women being silent in church: "Women should remain silent in the churches. They are not allowed to speak, but must be in submission, as the Law says. If they want to inquire about something, they should ask their own husbands at home; for it is disgraceful for a woman to speak in the church" (1 Cor 14:34-35).

Why does Paul give instructions on the proper dress for women who pray and prophesy in public and then turn around and tell them to be silent? Was the great apostle inconsistent?

# CHAPTER SIX

# Paul
# and
# Women

**M**Y MOTHER USED TO compare the situation in Corinth to the one she and my father faced in northern China. Back in the 1920s when they were the first to bring God's message to that forgotten area, they found women with bound feet who seldom left their homes and who, unlike the men, had never in their whole lives attended a public meeting or a class. They had never been told as little girls, "Now you must sit still and listen to the teacher." Their only concept of an assembly was a family feast where everyone talked at once.

When these women came to my parents' church and gathered on the women's side of the sanctuary, they thought this was a chance to catch up on the news with their neighbors and to ask questions about the story of Jesus they were hearing. Needless to say, along with babies crying and toddlers running about, the women's section got rather noisy! Add to that the temptation for the women to shout questions to their husbands across the aisle, and you can imagine the chaos. As my mother patiently tried to tell the women that they should listen first and chitchat or ask questions later, she would mutter under her breath, "Just like Corinth; it just couldn't be more like Corinth."

## The Problem in Corinth

When Paul wrote 1 Corinthians 14:34-35 the women of that day did not stop prophesying in public meetings. Paul, it seems, was telling them how to behave while *others* were speaking; he was not prohibiting *them* from sharing. A closer look at the Greek words used may help.

The Greek word *sigaō,* translated "silent" (v. 34), is also used in Acts 12:17; 15:12 and 21:40. In these situations people were to be quiet and give their attention to the speaker. The Greek word *laleō* (v. 34) is translated "speak." While the New Testament most often uses *laleō* to refer to ordinary speech, including the preaching of the gospel, in the Greek literature of that period the word was sometimes used for gossip or prattle.[1] *Laleō* is used for those who talk a lot, but will not listen. That was the problem of the uneducated women in pre-Mao China. They had never been taught to listen. Plutarch was familiar with such a problem when he contrasted *laleō* with listening: "A man who talks [*lalounti*] to those who will not listen, and will not listen when others talk [*lalounton*]."[2]

If we allow that Paul may have been using the word in the sense of babble or inattentive talking, the passage would imply that the problems in Corinth were similar to those my parents faced in China. Paul was not taking away the freedom to pray and prophesy which is implied in 1 Corinthians 11:5, but he is dealing with excesses which occurred as a result of that freedom. In the process of determining the letter of the law in 1 Corinthians 14:34, we should not miss the spirit of the epistle, which expresses freedom while trying to correct libertinism.

Catherine and Richard Kroeger, furthermore, make the connection between verse 32: "The spirits of prophets are subject to the control of prophets" and the phrase in verse 34: "but they [women] must be in submission, as the Law says." The Kroegers point out that

although the translations are rarely the same, the same Greek verb is used in both verses 32 and 34. *Hupotassō,* meaning to arrange or place under, is in the middle voice, indicating that the person does this to him or herself. The concept of self-control is brought out in most translations of verse 32. . . . When the subject is so clearly self-control, how can the same verb be translated differently in the very same passage when it applies to women? Quite literally, verse 34 reads, "Let them [women] control themselves as the law also says."[3]

It has to this point been assumed that the *Law* referred to the Old Testament Law. But the Kroegers suggest, since there is no such law in the Old Testament tradition, that the words refer to the law made by the Gentiles:

As women's behavior tended to be far wilder than that of men, such legislation had been enacted in both Greek and Roman society. According to Plutarch's *Lives,* Solon, in conjunction with Epimenides (an expert in ecstatic religion), had established laws aimed at curbing the cultic excesses of women. . . . While biblical scholars have vainly searched for such a law in Jewish tradition, there is considerable evidence that every legal effort was made to control ecstatic feminine behavior in Greco-Roman society. . . . It was important to the early church that the behavior of their women should be above reproach and within the bounds of the law.[4]

Because of the Greco-Roman laws against women's religious excesses, it becomes easier to see that self-control, rather than silence, is the theme of this passage.

Paul finishes his instructions to women in 1 Corinthians 14:34-35 by suggesting that they ask questions of their husbands at home. We have already discussed how disruptive uneducated women were in pre-Mao China because they conversed with their friends and asked their husbands questions. Paul may have been giving a common-sense suggestion to the Corinthian women to hold their many questions until they got home.

But the apostle may have had another good reason for such a suggestion. It is hard for us to imagine the impoverished relationship that existed between husbands and wives in Greek society of the time. A wife would seldom think of discussing religion with her husband.

In order to insure that the children the wife bore were the husband's offspring, the wife was usually secluded in the women's quarters of the house. She was regarded as the property of the husband, and taking her out in public was considered improper. Therefore, the husband had to find intellectual female companionship from cultured and educated girlfriends, or *hetairai*. As Demosthenes explains, "We have hetairai for the pleasures of the spirit, concubines for sensual pleasure, and wives to give us sons."[5] And Socrates once questioned a man: "Is there anyone to whom you commit more affairs of importance than you commit to your wife?"

"There is not."

"Is there anyone with whom you talk less?"

"There are few or none, I confess."[6]

Paul may have been trying to encourage a higher degree of communication between husbands and wives by telling wives to ask questions at home. Unfortunately, Paul does not make his reasons explicit. We can only surmise that the apostle who wrote 1 Corinthians 13 would desire to see loving communication between spouses, especially when the women were eager to learn more about Jesus.

One of the many women who have tried to give a positive explanation to this passage is Jessie Penn-Lewis of England (1861-1927). Well known among missionaries of the China Inland Mission, she was one of the women whose biographies gripped me as a teen-ager in prison. I was fascinated with her love for the Lord, her encouraging message of victory for Christians, and her opportunities to minister in England, Sweden, Russia, Finland, India, Canada and the United States. Through her travels, her life was linked with people such as F. B. Meyer, Andrew Murray and D. L. Moody.

Two of her books which inspired me most in prison were her work on the Song of Solomon as an allegory of our love relationship with Jesus Christ and her book *Face to Face*. Here she described the love between God and Moses who spoke "face to face, as a man speaks with his friend" (Ex 33:11).

I did not know about *The Magna Charta of Woman*, published in England in 1919, until Bethany Fellowship brought it to the United States in 1975. In this book, Penn-Lewis deplores the fact that "so large a proportion of the women in Christendom are given over to fashion and folly" because they have not been given responsibility for the advancement of God's kingdom. And this, she says, is because of three passages in Paul's epistles that have been translated "in such a way that they have entirely misinterpreted the teaching of the Apostle."[7] The three passages referred to are 1 Corinthians 11:2-16; 14:34-35 and 1 Timothy 2: 8-15.[8]

### Instructions to Timothy
The exact meaning of Paul's letter to Timothy, as it affects women, is not very clear. Paul says in 1 Timothy 2:11-15:

A woman should learn in quietness and full submission.
I do not permit a woman to teach or to have authority
over a man; she must be silent. For Adam was formed
first, then Eve. And Adam was not the one deceived; it
was the woman who was deceived and became a sinner.
But women will be kept safe through childbirth, if they
continue in faith, love and holiness with propriety.

As in the 1 Corinthians passage, Paul here seems to be con-
tradicting his own assumption that women will pray and
prophesy in the church. What can he mean?

Berkeley Mickelsen of Bethel Seminary believes that
Paul was trying to correct a situation where false teaching
had gotten out of hand. He writes:

False teaching is so deceptive that even a sinless woman
like Eve was defeated and deceived by [it]. Therefore,
be learning in quietness. . . . The situation in Ephesus
was not one in which Paul wanted women to try out their
wings and see how well they could teach. . . . So 1 Tim. 2:
11-15 was a regulation for women where they were. Today it is a regulation for both sexes if they have not made
careful preparation to meet false teaching.[9]

Here Mickelsen distinguishes between a rule which applies
to one particular situation and a general principle which
would apply to all times and places.

Catherine and Richard Kroeger offer another possible
interpretation. They have unearthed evidence which sheds
a great deal of light on these verses. Although their conclu-
sions have yet to be widely evaluated by other scholars, I
believe their argument deserves consideration here.

The problem all along has been that *authentein* (v. 12)
appears nowhere else in the New Testament and only very
rarely in other Greek literature. We therefore have had few
clues as to its meaning. The Kroegers make a strong case
for translating *authentein* as "to involve someone in solicit-
ing sexual liaisons" rather than as "to usurp authority,

domineer, or exercise authority over." (Berkeley Mickelsen also acknowledges that *authentein* is a rare verb with vulgar connotations.)

The Kroegers build their case from uses of *authentein* in Greek literature from the period preceding the New Testament.[10] But why would Paul have to tell Timothy that women should not solicit sexual favors? As unlikely as it may seem, this was apparently a major problem within the early church. Both the churches at Pergamum and Thyatyra were condemned for teaching sexual immorality (Rev 2:14, 20). Peter also condemned people within the church who were leading others into sexual immorality (2 Pet 2:14, 18). The Kroegers find evidence for sexually immoral behavior among various religious groups in the Wisdom of Solomon, where "cursed children" are mentioned along with *authentein*. These "cursed children" are presumed to be the offspring of immoral liaisons. Clement of Alexandria complained about Christian groups who had turned the communion service into a sex orgy, and he calls people who participated in this form of religion *authentai*. Throughout the Greco-Roman world, it seems there were groups—some of them calling themselves Christian—which combined worship, teaching and sexual immorality.[11]

Related to these various cults and misguided Christian groups were the heresies which posited that women possessed superior intellectual and spiritual knowledge and priority in creation. Many of these heresies suggested that Eve was created first and in turn gave life and knowledge to Adam.

Ephesus was a center for such spiritual cults, so it is not unlikely that Paul was writing in reference to these when he wrote to Timothy.[12] This would also explain his concern for modest dress and behavior and quiet demeanor. If Paul is indeed responding to the "female" heresies, then his statements about creation make a great deal of sense. In

verses 13 and 14 he is giving a précis of the creation account
in order to dispute directly the assertion that Eve was the
morally and spiritually superior being. Paul makes it clear
that Eve did not have superior knowledge but was herself
deceived, and sinned.[13]

In this context also, Paul's statement about a woman's
being kept safe through childbirth begins to make sense.
He is indicating that even if women have borne illegitimate
children because of their participation in these cultic activities, they will be saved if they repent in faith and continue
in love and holiness.[14]

According to the Kroegers' suggested translation of *authentein,* 1 Timothy 2:12 should read: "I do not permit a
woman to teach sexual immorality or to involve a man
in sexual activity."

## A Balance between Extremes

Paul's statements to women are best viewed in both the
cultural and biblical contexts in which they appear. In the
society of that day, women had few rights and very little
respect as persons. Against this the gospel declared that
men and women are one in Christ and heirs of the promise (Gal 3:28). Paul knew of the women models of the
Gospels: that the first to know about the Incarnation were
Mary and Elizabeth (Lk 1:29-45); that among the first to
understand that Jesus must die for the world was Mary of
Bethany, since she anointed Jesus for his burial (Jn 12:1-8).
Paul also probably had heard that Jesus revealed himself
as the Messiah to the woman of Samaria (Jn 4:25-26) and
that Martha had confessed to Jesus, "I believe that you are
the Christ, the Son of God, who was to come into the world"
(Jn 11:27).

Furthermore, Paul knew personally of the activity of
women in the early church. Michael Green sums up the
situation:

A glance through the Acts [confirms] this impression of the significant part played by women in the spread of the gospel: Dorcas, Lydia, Priscilla, the four prophesying daughters of Philip whose fame was widespread in the second century, the upper-class women of Beroea and Thessalonica, and the rest. The Epistles confront us with a deaconess, possibly even a female apostle! Eight of the twenty-six people mentioned in the greetings in Romans 16 are women, and the rivalries of women workers in evangelism are rebuked in Philippians 4. The part played by women is all the more remarkable in view of the fact that in Jewish circles and in paganism alike it was very much a man's world.... Yet these same women were among the most successful evangelists.[15]

Paul, like Peter and the other apostles, learned firsthand that not just Jews, but also Gentiles, slaves, free people and women were called to serve Christ Jesus.

### The Church in the '80s

If Rip Van Winkle had gone to sleep in the second century and awakened in ours, he would have seen some changes for the better. However, if he had known intimately the life of the early church, he might be surprised at the lack of female leadership in many churches, the separation between inner-city churches for the poor and suburban churches for the rich, and the tendency for each racial group to have its own services, whether they use the dominant language of the country in which they live or not.

That same first love that was lost in the church at Ephesus according to John's Revelation is still lacking in the church today. And the same Holy Spirit that called the Ephesian Christians to repentance comes to us also. Perhaps we have been too busy listening to other voices to hear the call. Why has the modern church neglected its responsibility to call *women* as well as men to fulfill the Great Commission? to put Christ, not a man, first in their lives? to serve as Phoebe, Priscilla and Lydia served?

Perhaps the modern church has focused on the Fall of the human race in the Garden of Eden. There the serpent tempted both the man and the woman to disobey God. Adam and Eve broke God's rules and ruined the perfect relationship between them and their Creator.

This story has been used to try to prove the superiority of men over women. Luther spoke for many theologians when he wrote, "The subtlety of satan showed itself also when he attacked human nature where it was weakest, namely, in Eve and not in Adam. I believe that had Satan first tempted the man, Adam would have gained the victory."[16] Of course, Luther inherited his prejudices from those who preceded him, such as Tertullian, Jerome, Augustine, Aquinas and many others. And preachers of our day suffer from the same teaching.

I sat in the St. Paul Civic Center in November 1978 and listened to a nationally known preacher tell us that Eve's problem was that she did not call Adam to the door to talk to the serpent. Among the thousands who turned out to hear this strange story, the majority were women. A depressing spell settled over the group, and I wondered how many of the women were single, widowed, divorced or married to a man who would be hard put if called upon to handle a temptation straight from the devil. We were made to feel that protection from Satanic attacks was limited to the few women who had husbands who took complete responsibility for their wives' spiritual welfare.

Another part of the Genesis story that has been used against women is the statement given to the woman that the man "will rule over you" (Gen 3:16). Helmut Thielicke points out that man's rule over woman "is not an imperative order of creation but rather the element of disorder that disturbs the original peace of creation."[17] It is a *prediction,* not a prescription. Yet some contemporary works, like *Fascinating Womanhood,* quote Genesis 3:16 as God's first commandment to women.[18]

It is interesting that *Fascinating Womanhood* has found its way into evangelical church libraries. Many men and women who would not go outside the orthodox evangelical tradition for help on other subjects are willing to do so in the area of women. This book, however, is written by someone who is not considered orthodox or evangelical and contains many ideas that are contrary to the teaching of Jesus Christ.

False teaching leads us into two sins: dethroning Jesus Christ as Lord and discriminating against the least of his brothers and sisters. We dethrone Jesus when we look for human answers to our problems. And when we accept human answers, we allow ourselves to be prejudiced against those who are different from us. How often has the Holy Spirit been quenched among people from the Third World, among those from a lower economic stratum of society, and among women because of prejudice and ignorance in the church? The promotional brochure for one large international conference held in Switzerland listed fourteen well-known male speakers, most of whom were white. In small print at the bottom of the page I read, "Leaders from the third world countries will also participate." Why were they not named and given a more prominent place on the program? And why were there no women speakers? When we ignore large segments of the body of Christ we are quenching the Holy Spirit.

Because of this danger, the late A. J. Gordon, for whom Gordon College and Gordon-Conwell Theological Seminary are named, said that the Spirit is not only in the Word, but the "spirit is also in the Church, the body of regenerate and sanctified believers." Gordon went on to illustrate how the Spirit works in the church by telling us that "in every great spiritual awakening in the history of Protestantism the impulse for Christian women to pray and witness for Christ in the public assembly has been found irrepressible."[19]

Gordon wrote almost a hundred years ago. Is his message also relevant to our day? Perhaps God will speak through women, slaves and people from all nations as promised on the day of Pentecost. Certainly he has spoken through women in the past, and perhaps we can learn from their examples.

# PART THREE

# A Cloud
of Women
Witnesses

# CHAPTER SEVEN

# Leaders in the Early Church: A.D. 100-500

THE HUMAN SAGA TELLS us that often love leads to death. Patriots die for the country they love, and lovers prefer death to separation. Today thousands are dying for the sake of their divine Lover. They come from Communist or Third-World countries, but they are part of us, and we are part of them because we love the same Lord.

It was Jesus who started this process of loving and dying. The One who went to the cross calls us to join our sisters in loving the Lord to the point of death. The One who loves us most asks us to return to the cross to share in the joy of the martyrs who "did not love their lives so much as to shrink from death" (Rev 12:11).

Edith Dean deals with the dilemma of love and death in *The Bible's Legacy for Womanhood:*

We never understand suffering until we have embraced

the Cross. . . . Women who ministered to [Jesus] and took
part in the formation of Christ's church carried many
crosses: opposition within their own ranks, imprison-
ment and martyrdom by the Roman Tribunal, the un-
truths about Christ and his Gospel, and the little with
which to do and so much to do, in order that his life and
message might illuminate the centuries.[1]
The first among this noble band of women were those who
traveled with Jesus in his earthly ministry (Lk 8:1-3). They
remained longest at the cross and arrived first at the empty
tomb. After the long vigil, Mary Magdalene ran to announce the greatest news of all history—that Jesus was
risen—only to be met with unbelief, perhaps partly because
Jewish men were taught not to trust the word of a woman.
When the disciples on the road to Emmaus shared the
women's unbelievable story with Jesus, he rebuked them,
"How foolish you are, and how slow of heart to believe all
that the prophets have spoken!" (Lk 24:25).

Thinking of these women's dedication to Jesus Christ,
the late Bishop Fulton Sheen asks:
Which stands up better in a crisis—man or woman? The
best way to arrive at a conclusion is to go to the greatest
crisis the world ever faced, namely, the Crucifixion of
our Divine Lord. When we come to this great drama of
Calvary, there is one fact that stands out very clearly.
Men failed . . . on the other hand, there is not one single
instance of a woman's failing him."[2]
This tradition of deep love and loyalty to Jesus continued
throughout the early-church period. Among the women
who traveled in Asia Minor preaching, Thecla was referred
to as "the first martyr." According to Basil, she won many to
Christ and baptized them. After severe persecution in
Iconium, she set up a teaching center in a cave near Seleu-
cia. Gregorium speaks of Thecla, along with Peter, Paul,
James, Stephen, Luke and Andrew, as contending for the

faith "with fire and sword, beasts and tyrants."[3]

Many women like Thecla were martyred for their love for Jesus in the first two centuries of Christianity. There was always a risk for those who spoke openly about him. Michael Green tells of "the almost superhuman dedication of which early Christian women were capable," and goes on to illustrate his point by telling of one who "went with dignity and courage to her death."[4]

He continues:

The Gallic slave girl, Blandina, died with just as much courage and fidelity to Christ as Perpetua, the aristocratic African lady. The moving story is told by eyewitnesses in Vienne in A.D. 177, and their letter was reproduced almost in full by Eusebius. She was a recent convert, and her mistress was fearful not for their lives, but lest Blandina should draw back in face of death. She need not have worried. Tortured with fiendish ingenuity, she quietly maintained, "I am a Christian woman, and nothing wicked happens among us." Put on the gridiron, thrown to wild beasts in the arena, forced to watch the murder of her Christian companions, impaled upon a stake, this remarkable girl, "weak and despised though she was, had put on the great invincible athlete, Christ, and through many contests gained the crown of immortality." She was finally dispatched by being put in a net and tossed by a bull; but not before she had nerved a fifteen-year-old boy, Ponticus, to martyrdom by her example, and had prayed lovingly and persistently for her persecutors. If women like this were at all typical throughout the varied social strata of the Church, it is hardly surprising that the gospel overcame the enormous obstacles in its way, and began to capture the Roman Empire.[5]

During the first two hundred years of church history, the expansion of the church happened through ordinary believers, both men and women, aristocrats and slaves. Blandina was a poor slave girl; Michael Green also mentioned the aristocratic Perpetua.

## Perpetua

Perpetua was a young married woman of noble birth and good education, who lived in Carthage, North Africa, and became a martyr. When she was tried before the procurator, he asked, "Art thou a Christian?"

"I am," she answered.

The rest of the story was written down by the twenty-two-year-old Perpetua herself:

> Then he passed sentence on the whole of us, and condemned us to the beasts; and in great joy we went down into the prison. Then because my baby was accustomed to take the breast from me, and stay with me in prison, I sent at once the deacon Pomponius to my father to ask for my baby. But my father refused to give him. And as God willed, neither had he any further wish for my breasts, nor did they become inflamed; that I might not be tortured by anxiety for the baby and pain in my breasts.

The day before the fight with the beasts, Perpetua dreamed of combat with a man:

> And I caught hold of his head, and he fell on his face; and I trod upon his head. And the people began to shout, and my supporters to sing psalms. And I came forward to the trainer, and received the bough. ... And I began to go in triumph to the Gate of Life. And I awoke. And I perceived that I should not fight with beasts but with the Devil; but I knew the victory to be mine.

The story is continued by Saturus, who was martyred with Perpetua. He also had a vision of heaven:

> The angels said unto us: "Come first and enter and greet the Lord." And we came near to a place whose walls were

built like as it might be of light. . . . And we entered, and
heard a sound as of one voice saying, "Holy, holy, holy,"
without ceasing. And we saw sitting in the same place one
like unto a man. . . . And entering we stood in wonder
before the throne; and the four angels lifted us up, and
we kissed Him, and He stroked our faces with His hand.
. . . And the elders said to us: "Go and play." And I said
to Perpetua: "You have your wish." And she said to me:
"Thanks be to God that as I was merry in the flesh, so am
I now still merrier here."
The story is finished by an unknown editor who might have
been Tertullian:
For the young women the Devil made ready a mad
heifer. . . . Perpetua was tossed first, and fell on her loins.
. . . Then, having asked for a pin, she further fastened
her disordered hair. For it was not seemly that a martyr
should suffer with her hair dishevelled, lest she should
seem to mourn in the hour of her glory. . . . Perpetua
was supported by a certain Rusticus, then a catechumen,
who kept close to her; and being roused from what
seemed like sleep, so completely had she been in the
Spirit and in ecstasy, began to look about her, and said
to the amazement of all: "When we are to be thrown to
that heifer, I cannot tell." When she heard what had already taken place, she refused to believe it till she had
observed certain marks of ill-usage on her body and
dress. Then she summoned her brother and spoke to
him and the catechumen, saying: "Stand ye all fast in the
faith, and love one another; and be not offended by our
sufferings."
[After climbing the ladder, Perpetua,] that she might
taste something of the pain, was struck on the bone and
cried out, and herself guided to her throat the wavering
hand of the young untried gladiator. Perhaps so great a
woman, who was feared by the unclean spirit, could not

otherwise be slain except she willed.[6]

This happened in March, A.D. 203. Such an example of devotion to Jesus Christ can only lead us to worship and adoration. By contrast, in the 1980s I am baffled when I meet women who are too shy to say even one sentence in honor of Jesus. "Oh, I just couldn't bring myself to say what I really wanted to say," one woman confided after a meeting. "You see, I have a bad heart," she added apologetically.

Others confess that they are too bashful to say a word in defense of Christ when, over a cup of coffee, a friend blames the Lord for all the evil people have brought on themselves and others through their sin.

### Santa Lucia

Santa Lucia of Sicily had no fears about the gospel. When I was a child we celebrated the Santa Lucia festival with our Swedish hosts in Taofungshan. At thirteen I had never felt more beautiful than I did in that long, white gown with my waist-length blonde hair held in place by a crown of ferns—with real lighted candles in it. I imagined I was an angel as I entered each dark bedroom of our Scandinavian compound to offer the Santa Lucia goodies, while my attendants sang the Santa Lucia song. I wished the event would never end.

The real Santa Lucia lived about A.D. 300 in Syracuse, Sicily, and became involved in Christian charitable work there. She was betrothed to a wealthy nobleman, but lost his favor when she refused to stop giving aid to the needy. Instead, she continued with greater fervor, actually giving away her wedding gifts. When she would not stop, the nobleman turned her over to the Roman prefect who placed her in jail. She was tortured and her eyes gouged with hot iron spears, but she would not renounce her faith in Christ. When her sight was miraculously restored, she was condemned to death by burning. This method, too, was unsuccessful and she miraculously lived. But in the end her life was taken by a "magic" sword.[7]

The first missionaries from Ireland brought the story of Santa Lucia to Sweden. There she became a symbol of the light of Christianity, and December 13—the darkest day of the year according to the old calendar—was chosen as the day to honor her. Her story is recorded in Swedish folk history.

After the persecutions suffered by Lucia and others, there came a time of peace. The Roman emperor Constantine was converted to Christianity in A.D. 312, and the Christian religion became not only respectable but a positive asset for those who sought the favor of the emperor.[8] As the church grew in size, it also grew in structure. Instead of clandestine, countercultural groups, the churches erected large, public meeting places, and developed more sophisticated forms of worship.

The free service, spelled out by Paul in 1 Corinthians 14:26-33, where by the Spirit believers shared tongues and prophecies and hymns, was slowly replaced by prepared liturgies. Instead of the whole church exercising spiritual gifts and taking part in the proclamation of the gospel, leadership fell into the hands of a chosen few who had specific intellectual preparation for such office.

The sting of these changes was not felt by women till years later. The shift was so gradual that they were hardly aware of what was happening. As long as many of the churches continued to meet in the homes of women, they still carried a significant responsibility within the Christian community. From the first, the women who opened their homes for house churches, like Lydia and the "elect lady" of 2 John, had obvious places of spiritual leadership among people whom they had probably been instrumental in leading to Christ and nurturing in the faith. Such households continued to be lighthouses for Jesus Christ as relatives, slaves, clients, and friends came to faith in the warm atmosphere of Christian house churches.

Some of these larger house churches became the sites of cathedrals and bishops' palaces. With women continuing to take leading parts in the worship services, the idea of an order for those who thus served slowly evolved. These women were first called deaconesses and later canonesses. As they were ordained to assist in the services of the cathedrals, they began to live together nearby. According to Joan Morris, an Oxford University lecturer, women were the first to live in community.[9] Also according to Morris, canonesses were considered to be of apostolic origin. Augustine wrote their rules and later adapted them for men.[10]

Some commentators believe 1 Timothy 5:3-16 describes the beginnings of an "order" of widows who served the church and were supported by it. Dorcas, a widow who is mentioned in Acts 9:36-43, may have been a member of this "order."[11]

Except for the orders, information has been scarce on the role of women in the church after the persecutions ceased. But in the past hundred years, the Roman catacombs have once more become a center of interest for Christian historians. In the "Cappella Greca" of the Catacomb of Priscilla, a second-century fresco has been found with seven women celebrating Holy Communion. On the table there are the chalice, the bread and the fish, symbolizing Jesus Christ. On either side are the baskets of bread as a reminder of the multiplication of the bread in the desert. All the seven people look very feminine except for the one to the left who might be a man, but the dress comes down to the ankles in the fashion of women of that time.

But were women permitted to administer Holy Communion? Athanasius affirmed that they were. In a document to a community of virgins in the fourth century, he said: "If there are two or three Virgins with you, let them

'Give Thanks' over the bread together with you." Then he
added that catechumens must leave, which is still the custom during Communion in the Greek Orthodox Church
today. Athanasius believed that virgins lived life as if they
were in heaven, and "in the kingdom of heaven there is
neither male nor female, so that women pleasing to the
Lord may receive the Order of men."[12]

Tombstones are another source of information on
women of this period. Dorothy Irvin of the College of St.
Catherine in St. Paul, Minnesota, cites two Greek-language
tombstones with these inscriptions: "The tomb of Ver-
onica (or approximately that name) the presbyter (feminine genitive) and daughter of Joses" and "The tomb of
Faustina the presbyter (feminine genitive). Shalom."[13]

While some women were presbyters, others found their
special place in the religious convents where they could
express their love and loyalty to Jesus Christ and find their
identity in that relationship, as did the virgins that Athanasius instructed. Sister Mary McKenna contrasts this
"place" with the lack of place for women in much of the
life of the church today. Though she speaks of the Roman
Catholic Church, her comments about a place for women
are relevant in many churches:

> The repressive, closed, defensive attitude toward women
> of our very male Church of today did not have a coun-
> terpart in the "primitive" Church in the Church of a
> period when, paradoxically, the sociological status of
> women was so much lower. What Christian women had
> then, and what is lacking today, is the status of ecclesial
> *order*, and the attendant sense of having a definite place
> and function in the Church's official structure.[14]

The idea of an order meant a life that combined contemplation with action. This had a great appeal to believers in the
early centuries. Helena Wiebe writes in "Women of God in
Early Christian Sodalities," "The early Christian Church

seemed to view life as a rehearsal for the coming of the Bride-groom, Jesus Christ. There was to be readiness and prepara-tion for the return, by faithful service and vigilance in re-sponsibility in the great family of the Kingdom of God."[15]

## The Ascetic Life
By the fourth century more and more women were attract-ed to the ascetic life of contemplation and prayer. Life for these women in the convents meant being liberated (from early marriage and heavy family responsibilities) for service to the kingdom.

Life in the convent offered a woman freedom to find her identity in her relationship to Christ and to develop that identity in a community that combined deep devotion to Christ with scholarship to the glory of God. Rosemary Ruether has pointed out that only "women dedicated to asceticism could count on the support of the Church in making decisions against their family's demands that they marry and bear children."[16]

One of the best-known ascetic women of the fourth cen-tury was Macrina who lived in Cappadocia (the area of present-day Turkey). As a teen-ager she refused her fam-ily's efforts to arrange a marriage for her. After her father's death, she also brought her mother into the ascetic life, and the family estate became a community for prayer and charitable works.

Macrina influenced her brother Basil when he returned from years of study abroad. According to another brother, Gregory, Bishop of Nyssa, she lured Basil "so quickly to the goal of philosophy that he withdrew from worldly show and began to look down upon acclaim through oratory and went over to this life full of labors for one's hand to per-form, providing for himself through complete poverty a mode of living that would without impediment lead to virtue."[17]

Later Macrina and Basil founded parallel communities for men and women. John Chrysostom, the great church father, wrote that Macrina "was a great organizer, an independent thinker, and as well-educated as Basil himself."[18] In her community for women, Macrina taught the Scriptures to anyone who would come and listen. She also established a hospital where divine healing was practiced. Many came to the community with both physical and spiritual needs. According to her brother Gregory, Macrina set an example of "no anger, jealousy, hatred, pride, luxuries or honors."[19] Together with the other women, Macrina sang and prayed unceasingly, expressing her love and gratitude to her God.

Macrina and Basil established their houses in the mountainous region of Pontus, overlooking the Iris River. At the same time, in Rome, the beautiful and wealthy Marcella founded the first community for women in the Western church. As a little girl, Marcella had listened to Athanasius, patriarch of Alexandria, tell about the monks who lived in the deserts of Egypt. She never forgot his words. When her husband died prematurely, she turned her mansion into a Christian retreat center.

In A.D. 392 the Bible translator Jerome arrived in Rome from Constantinople to attend a church council and was assigned as a guest to the hospitality of Marcella. She persuaded him to hold Bible classes for some of Rome's most distinguished women. Jerome in turn persuaded the women to study Hebrew so they could read the Old Testament in the original text. Marcella took the challenge, and for years wrote him letters asking about difficulties in the translation of words like *selah, ephod* and *teraphim.* Jerome once complained that he had been up all night dictating answers to her detailed questions.[20]

But for the first three years of their friendship, Jerome stayed in Rome and worked on his translation of the whole

Bible into the Latin version, the Vulgate, which became the Bible of Christendom for a thousand years. As he taught the Bible to his hostess and her friends, he also says he profited from their criticism. About Marcella he also wrote, "What had come to me as the fruit of long study and constant meditation [his Latin translation of the Bible], she learned and made it her own."[21]

Because of the Bible classes he conducted there, Jerome later called Marcella's place *Ecclesia Domestica,* "the Church of the Household." As a center for prayer, study and Christian charity, this "church" inspired Fabiola to found one of the world's first hospitals in Rome. And Paula and her daughter Eustochium decided to dedicate their lives to helping Jerome with his Bible translation. They later joined him in Bethlehem for this purpose.[22] Meanwhile, Marcella established the first convent for women on the outskirts of Rome.

After Jerome left Rome, he often advised his friends there to get materials on the Bible from Marcella. Once when there was a dispute in Rome over the meaning of Scripture, he asked Marcella to settle it. Commenting on her influence, Jerome wrote, "I had the joy of seeing Rome transformed into another Jerusalem."[23] He was especially happy with the group of women who joined Marcella in the convent, giving themselves to prayer, Bible study, singing of psalms in Hebrew and caring for the poor. Jerome said her delight in Scripture was incredible. Marcella loved to sing, "Thy words have I hid in my heart that I might not sin against thee," and the psalm that described the perfect person as one whose "delight is in the law of the Lord and in His law doth he meditate day and night." Jerome said that Marcella understood this act of meditation as something requiring action. In one letter she asked him: What are the things which an eye has not seen nor ear heard? (1 Cor 2:9). Jerome answered that these are spiritual things which can only be spiritually discerned.[24]

When the Goths invaded Rome in 410, Marcella was eighty-five years old. They beat her with whips, but she said she felt no pain. Jerome related that Christ must have softened their hearts because they finally let Marcella and a friend go to the Basilica of St. Paul, which was used then as a refuge for the poor. Thanking God for deliverance and for the fact that the Goths had found her poor, she died at the Basilica a few days later, knowing that true wealth is of the spirit.

Marcella was among the great cloud of women witnesses who knew Jesus Christ as their Lord and Savior—women like Melania, whom Jerome hailed as a "new Thecla." She founded the first monastery on the Mount of Olives.

Melania's granddaughter, Melania Junior, friend of both Jerome and Augustine, followed in her footsteps and was famous for her missionary journeys. Coming from a wealthy family in Rome with estates all around the Mediterranean, Melania Junior used her resources to give to the poor and to build monasteries and churches for both men and women in Africa and Jerusalem. It was on a trip to Africa that she took on the severe disciplines of fasting and prayer, and studied intensely both Scripture and the lives of the desert fathers.[25]

On one journey, Melania Junior went to Constantinople for an imperial wedding and used the opportunity to instruct a circle of prominent women against the heresy of Nestorius. At the same time, she was instrumental in the conversion of her uncle Volusian, an influential man at the court. She also inspired the Empress Eudocia to make a pilgrimage to Jerusalem.

But perhaps the most outstanding contribution of Melania to church history is her emphasis on praising God. On two separate occasions, she built monasteries "where a community of monks could chant perpetual praises" to their

Lord.[26] This emphasis on praise is reminiscent of the Old
Testament where we find singers in both the tabernacle
and the Temple that "were employed in that work day and
night" (1 Chron 6:31-32; 9:33; Ezra 2:41, 65; Neh 7:1).
Melania's followers could be compared to "the singers unto
the LORD . . . that should praise the beauty of holiness [say-
ing], 'Praise the LORD; for his mercy endureth for ever' "
(2 Chron 20:21 KJV). To sing praises to God was one important way for Melania to declare to the world who was
her first loyalty.

Significantly, Melania started her missionary journeys
after fleeing Rome during the invasion by the Goths in 410.
With the fall of Rome the gospel was forcibly spread by
refugees to all parts of Europe and the known world. In
this great missionary movement, women always played an
important role. Many of the women who brought the
gospel to my northern European ancestors came as hos-
tages who later married their captors and evangelized
them.

This form of evangelism has been common throughout
history. One story of a wife who won her husband to Christ
comes to us from the time of Pope Boniface. In A.D. 625
the pope wrote to Queen Ethelberga of England, whose
husband, King Edwin, was still a pagan:

Our paternal responsibility moves us to urge Your Christian Majesty, imbued with the force of divine inspiration,
not to avoid the duty imposed on us in season and out of
season, in order that, with the assistance and strength of
our Lord and Savior Jesus Christ, the King also may be
added to the Christian fold. . . . My illustrious daughter,
persevere in using every effort to soften his heart by
teaching him the commandments of God. Help him to
understand . . . the marvellous worth of the reward that
you have been accounted worthy to receive in this new
birth. Melt the coldness of his heart by teaching him

80110

about the Holy Spirit, so that the warmth of divine faith may set his mind on fire through your constant encouragement.... If you do this, the witness of the Holy Spirit will most certainly be fulfilled in you, that, "the unbelieving husband shall be saved through the believing wife." ... We beg you to inform us ... what measure of success God's goodness grants you in the conversion of your husband and the people over whom you reign.... And when we see the glory of the divine atonement spreading ever more widely among you, we shall give glad and heartfelt thanks to God, the Giver of all good things."[27]

Ethelberga was the daughter of Ethelbert, the first Christian king of Kent, and Bertha, who started the first center of Christian worship at Canterbury. Her mother taught Ethelberga to love God. Therefore, it was not surprising that two years after the pope's letter, King Edwin was baptized. Baptized at the same time was Hilda, his niece, who was brought up as a Christian by the queen. Many others in the family were also converted because of Ethelberga.

Soon after his conversion, King Edwin was killed while fighting to spread the faith. His niece was profoundly impressed by a king who was willing to die for Christ, and she decided to devote her life to God's service. When Edwin's successor wanted to start Christian centers, she was ready to help.

When I first came across this beautiful letter from Pope Boniface to Ethelberga, I wondered who was living in the "dark ages"—the queen and the pope, or those who today advise Christian women not to discuss Christ with their unbelieving husbands.

# *CHAPTER EIGHT*

# Sustaining the Faith through the Middle Years: 600-1700

AMONG THE GREAT CLOUD of women witnesses who call to us over the span of the ages are the women who founded or reformed the orders that kept Christianity alive through the Middle Ages. In England, Hilda of Whitby (614-80) was asked by the king and by Bishop Aidan of Iona to help start the first monasteries in the kingdom. She is best known for the community of nuns and monks she organized to live around the communal church in Whitby. The Venerable Bede tells us in his *Ecclesiastical History* that she insisted that future clergy be trained in the holy Scriptures. Five of her disciples became famous bishops.[1]

In the field of English letters, Hilda is remembered for having discovered and trained Caedmon, the first English poet to express his faith in the Anglo-Saxon language.

Poetry became a new vehicle for communicating the gospel
to the common people. Caedmon's poems started with the
story of creation and may have inspired Milton to write
*Paradise Lost.*

Along with other eminent abbesses, Hilda had the
powers of a baron, sitting on governing boards, furnishing
soldiers in time of war, and reporting directly to the king.
In ecclesiastical affairs she was directly under the pope.[2]
The Venerable Bede summed up Hilda's life: "She never
failed to return thanks to her Maker or publicly or pri-
vately to instruct the flock committed to her charge."[3] She
died in 680 while instructing her disciples to keep unity
within the church.

### Helpers of the Poor
While Hilda was a pioneer when Christianity was just taking
root, Clare (1194-1253) worked much later. She was a re-
former where Christianity had forgotten the poor, and she
founded the Franciscan order of barefoot nuns in Italy.
A number of princesses joined the Poor Clares—as they
were called—among them Agnes, the daughter of the king
of Bohemia. With seven other women of nobility, Agnes set
up the first convent in Prague.

Another king's daughter, Elisabeth of Hungary, took
her vows in 1228 and became the first Franciscan sister in
Germany. She served lepers, the aged and the poor, and
talked with God as she spun wool for her livelihood. She
was only twenty-four when she died, but the Church of St.
Elisabeth, built in her memory, is the greatest monument in
the world to any Christian woman.[4]

Another woman who revitalized the church was Catherine of Siena (1347-80). She humbly served the sick and
dying when the Black Death swept Europe, and she forth-
rightly called kings, queens and the pope to repent and
get right with God. Eleanor McLaughlin writes about her:

Catherine was truly selfless in her capacity to identify in genuine humility with the sinner. She persuaded the Pope to share in her sense of sin by walking barefoot, an act of papal penitence never done before or repeated since. She was at the same time inflamed by a passionate vision of goodness, of the Church reformed, of the righteousness of God's will, and irresistible passion for the salvation of those persons she addressed. Her hatred of sin was combined with a love for the sinner. . . . Her ideal, her vision of holiness, her Holy Desire for God was a gift of contemplation which forced her and all who heard her into action for love of neighbor and reform of the Church."[5]

As she contemplated God's love seen in the crucified Christ, Catherine's response was one of zeal to honor God and save souls. The love that embraced the cross and issued in action was combined with obedience—"a radical, world-ignoring attachment to Jesus and God's will for her."[6]

She encouraged others to seek the same love relationship with Jesus Christ: "Fear and serve God with no regard to thyself; and then do not care for what people may say. . . . Beware that thou lose thee nowhere but on the Cross, and there thou shalt find thyself more perfectly." And while urging a group of hermits to join her reform she wrote:

Lukewarmness proceeds from ingratitude, which comes from a faint light that does not let us see the agonizing and utter love of Christ crucified. . . . For in truth, did we see them, our heart would burn with the flame of love, and we should be *famished for time,* using it with great zeal for the honor of God and the salvation of souls. To this zeal I summon thee, dear son, that now we begin to work anew.[7]

Catherine was overcome by the wonder of God's love in the passion of Christ. To her it seemed impossible that a vision of that love should not result in human transforma-

tions and acts of love. She had the same expectations for
the church. Like the Reformers, she was aware of all the sins
of the church. Her call was constantly a call to repentance.
But unlike the Reformers, she remained obedient to
church authority. She was like the Bishop of Canterbury
who in the thirteenth century wrote to Pope Innocent IV:
"As an obedient son, I disobey, I contradict, I rebel."[8] Such
obedience carried with it a potential for reform.

For the most part during this time, women found the
outlets they needed within Church structures: "Before the
sixteenth century, it was in the Church, not in the sects,
that women found the most enduring and powerful roles.
Rebellion in the context of obedience, the vocation of the
saint, provided more space for women than did sectarian
protest."[9]

**Reformers**
For women, the Protestant Reformation meant one step
forward and one step backward. For many, the "just shall
live by faith" sounded like music to their ears. But the Ref
ormation affected women in some negative ways too
Arthur Glasser of Fuller Seminary writes:
> One of the tragedies of Protestantism is that it drove
> women from the cloistered life. True, to the 16th cen-
> tury reformers, this life appeared altogether harmful.
> But by their rendering all sodality structures [ecclesias-
> tical communities] invalid—which contributed so griev-
> ously to the absence of Protestant missionary outreach
> for more than 200 years—the reformers also subjected
> women to the confining perspective that their only
> recognized vocation was marriage. With the dissolution
> of the nunneries women lost their last chance of churchly
> service outside the narrow circle of husband, home and
> children.[10]

After Luther's attack on ecclesiastical authority, nuns and

monks by great numbers throughout Europe grew restless and decided to leave the monasteries. For instance, Katherine Von Bora with eight other nuns chose to break with the cloistered life and escaped at midnight in the empty barrels that had delivered herring to their Cistercian cloister near the border of Saxony. Luther and the herring merchant helped them at the risk of the death penalty. By leaving the convent, Katherine Von Bora and other women lost the accepted ecclesiastical framework from which they could proclaim the gospel. Von Bora later married Luther, whose views on the inferiority of women are well known.

The Reformers as a whole held that women existed for the comfort and well-being of men. Calvin explained what type of woman he most desired: "a woman who is gentle, pure, modest, economical, patient, and who is likely to interest herself about my health."[11] He was not concerned to find a woman who would have a ministry in her home or beyond it.

### Quakers

There were, however, isolated groups that began to question the limited role of women in the proclamation of the gospel. One of these groups was the Quakers in England. In 1657 a Quaker woman was arrested in front of her accuser, the parish priest of Hawkchurch. In answer to her inquiry about what crime she had committed, the priest answered, "A woman must not speak in the church." The rest of the story is recorded in *First Publishers of the Truth:* "So in conclusion they ordered her to go back to Hawkchurch that Night, and there she was to be whipt until the Blood did come, which was done the next Morning Early, she receiving many Cruell, bloody stripes."[12]

Women such as this had been inspired by the teaching of George Fox, founder of the Society of Friends, on the "priesthood of all believers" and by the opportunities given to men and women in the Quaker meetings to speak if they felt "the leading of the Spirit." When the King James Version made the Bible accessible to all English-speaking people in 1611, there was a new interest among the laity in reading and discussing its truths.

In their biblical study the Quakers found many areas of life that they believed needed change. Because all persons are equal before God, they refused to use titles for ecclesiastical or temporal authority figures. Furthermore, their belief in equality led to no distinctions between the sexes in the corporate life of the Christian community. In contrast to this, George Fox describes the treatment of one woman in a meeting where several Protestant groups were gathered: "At last one woman asked a question out of Peter, what that birth was, viz., a being 'born again of incorruptible seed, by the Word of God, that liveth and abideth forever.' And the priest said to her, 'I permit not a woman to speak in the church;' though he had before given liberty for any to speak."[13] The Quakers also refused to swear oaths because this would imply a lower standard of honesty for ordinary conversation. And in turbulent times, when England's Charles I had just been beheaded, they refused to take arms. The Quakers insisted on freedom of conscience at a time when religious groups persecuted each other for being different.[14]

Since the Quakers believed there were many weaknesses in the professional ministry, some of the women felt called to speak to those training for the ministry. They believed that the seminary men needed to know more about the life and work of Christ. In 1653, Mary Fisher and Elizabeth Williams went to Cambridge University and talked about the things of God with young theologians at the gate of Sidney College. For this the mayor of Sussex had them stripped naked to the waist and scourged. According to the records of Joseph Besse on Quaker sufferings from 1650-89, "in the midst of their punishment [they] sang and rejoiced, saying: 'The Lord be blessed, the Lord be praised, who hath thus honored us, and strengthened us to suffer for His name's sake.' "[15]

Another report relates that the two women said to their torturer, "If you think you have not done enough, we are here ready to suffer more for our Savior Christ." And then they knelt down and prayed, "Lord, lay not this sin to their charge."[16]

The news of the unmerciful flogging sent shudders throughout the country. But it did not keep Elizabeth Fletcher and Elizabeth Leavens from also going to witness to young theologians at Oxford University. These women were engaged in semipublic debates at a time in history when public debates were common. Almost any man could stand on a street corner and give his views on a subject to anyone who would stop and listen. The women were not asking for any special favors. They did not want to become ordained ministers, nor did they want any other recognition. All they wanted was the right to follow the promptings of the Holy Spirit to proclaim the Word of God. But the men at Oxford were not any more ready for the Word of God spoken by a woman than the men at Cambridge had been.

The women's confrontation in 1654 is described in *The First Publishers of the Truth:*

They suffered by the black tribe of scholars—for they dragged them first through a dirty pool, afterwards had them to a pump, and holding their mouths to the pump, endeavored to pump water thereinto with other shameful abuses; after threw the said Elizabeth Fletcher down upon a grave stone . . . and bruised her so sore that she never recovered it.[17]

George Fox tried to explain men's reaction to women preachers by saying that perhaps they felt threatened. But men "need not fear anyone's getting over them, for the power and Spirit of God gives liberty to all," said Fox.[18]

While in prison for refusing to swear an oath to the Commonwealth, Fox's wife, Margaret Fell Fox, wrote a pamphlet: "Women's Speaking Justified." There she claimed that Paul's admonition for women to be silent was written for a group of untrained women who were recently converted from paganism; to mature women Paul wrote instructions for praying and prophesying in public. With such encouragement Quaker women not only traveled all over England preaching, but ventured all the way to the New World.

In 1656, Ann Austin and Mary Fisher were arrested on arrival in the Massachusetts Bay colony. The treatment did not surprise Mary Fisher, who, after her flogging at Cambridge, was imprisoned for speaking to a priest in her home town. In Boston the hundred books she and her companion brought to the New World were burned, while the women were stripped naked, searched for marks of witchcraft and jailed to await deportation back to England. They would have starved in the Boston prison if an old man had not bribed the jailer to bring them food.

The Quaker women who followed them received even worse treatment. Finally, Elizabeth Hooton, a godly woman who had preached for years with the Baptists before she joined the Quakers, arrived in Boston for the second time with written permission from King Charles to purchase land for a home. But the Puritans ignored her royal permit and made the seventy-year-old missionary walk to Cambridge, Watertown and Dedham tied to a cart. In each town she was brought to the whipping post, stripped to the waist and beaten. Finally, she said, "They put me on a horse and carried me into ye wildernesse many miles, where was many wild beasts both bears and wolves and many deep waters where I waded through . . . but ye Lord delivered me."[19] This brave woman survived, returned to England, and later joined George Fox on a missionary journey to Jamaica where she finally died.

Elizabeth Hooten was not the only Quaker woman with a missionary vision. After Mary Fisher and Ann Austin took the Quaker message to Massachusetts in 1656 and were deported, Fisher set out from England for Turkey with five other missionaries. After landing in Greece, she proceeded alone to Turkey. William Sewel, a Quaker historian, tells of her arrival at the court of the Sultan in Adrianople:

> The Sultan bade her speak the word of the Lord to them, and not to fear, for they had good hearts and could hear it.... Then she spoke what was upon her mind. The Turks hearkened to her.... Then the Sultan desired her to stay in the country, saying that they could not but respect such a one, as should take so much pains to come to them so far as from England, with a message from the Lord God. He also proffered her a guard to bring her into Constantinople.... She, having no more to say, the Turks asked her what she thought of their prophet Mahomet and she answered she knew him not, but Christ the true prophet, the Son of God, who was the Light of the World, and enlightened every man coming to the world, Him, she knew.[20]

Though it took the Protestant church two hundred years after the Reformation before it seriously responded to the Great Commission, Mary Fisher was obedient to God and became a forerunner of the modern missionary movement to the Muslims.

### The Wesleyan Movement

The greatest breakthrough in opportunities for women to proclaim the gospel came with the Wesleyan revival in England in the eighteenth century. As in the days of the early church, the revivals brought repentance from old

prejudices, and new attitudes came with the new clean
hearts.

God's special instruments during these revivals were
Charles and John Wesley and George Whitefield. But long
before Charles and John were born, God touched their
mother, Susannah Wesley, and called her to a special ministry. Maybe Samuel Wesley, an Anglican minister, got
more than he bargained for when he married a woman
who, like Catherine of Sienna, self-consciously combined
the active and the contemplative life. Edith Dean writes
about Susannah Wesley, "Though she gave birth to nine-
teen children in the years between 1690 and 1709 . . . she set
aside two hours of each day for private devotion. . . . No
matter what intervened, at the stroke of the clock, she re-
tired to spiritual communion."[21]

Her son John, founder of the Methodist movement,
could never forget the sermons he heard his mother preach
to family members and neighbors on Sunday evenings
while her husband was on the Continent. As the crowds
became too big for her kitchen, the two hundred people
spread throughout the whole house and barn. While
Susannah Wesley made the conversion of her children her
prime concern, she believed God also wanted her to reach
beyond her own home.

But not every parishioner in her husband's church ap-
preciated this vision. Some wrote to her husband, complaining that she was going beyond the role of a woman.
When he asked her about this, she wrote,

> As I am a woman, so I am also mistress of a large family;
> and . . . in your absence, I cannot but look upon every
> soul you leave under my care, as a talent committed to
> me under a trust, by the great Lord of all the families,
> both of heaven and earth. . . . I cannot conceive why any
> should reflect upon you, because your wife endeavors to
> draw people to church, and to restrain them from pro-

faning the Lord's Day by this account. . . . As to its looking particular, I grant it does. And so does almost anything that is serious, or that may in any way advance the
glory of God, or the salvation of souls."[22]
It is not surprising that from such a home came two men
who changed the course of English history. What a thrill
it must have been for Susannah to stand by John as he
preached to twenty thousand people at once. Some historians have suggested that England did not have to go
through a revolution as dreadful as the French Revolution
because of the social changes that resulted from the Wesleyan revivals.[23] It was the revivals, not the Reformation,
that saved England.

The revivals in England and the Great Awakening in
America also changed people's attitudes about women proclaiming the good news. Through the revivals, women were
given the place that the Reformation had failed to give
them. When men and women repented of their sins before
a holy and righteous God and were open to the teaching of
the Holy Spirit on any subject, the status of women was
suddenly no longer an issue. Under the Spirit's anointing,
barriers of sex, class and race were lowered.

In such a climate, it was easy for John Wesley to follow
his mother's teaching and appoint women as local preachers and itinerant ministers. At first he did so cautiously by
suggesting that women give five-minute expositions on
Scripture. But then a crisis arose. His leading evangelist
died suddenly, and the evangelist's wife, Sarah Millett, was
taking care of his parish. In fact, she was preaching to
crowds as large as two or three thousand people. She was
also very well able to defend herself:

Now I do not apprehend that Mary could in the least be
accused of immodesty when she carried the joyful news
of the Lord's resurrection, and in that sense she taught
the teachers of mankind. Neither was the woman of Sa-

maria to be accused of immodesty when she invited the whole city to come to Christ. Neither do I suppose that Deborah did wrong publicly declaring the message of God.[24]

When in 1787, ten years later, the issue was raised about whether or not Sarah Millett should be officially recognized as a Methodist minister, what could John Wesley do but give her the right hand of fellowship?

Not everyone was happy about the breakdown of sex and class barriers. Lady Huntington was an upper-class friend of Wesley's who received a letter from the duchess of Buckingham asking about the new preachers. The duchess was not too happy about the answer she received from Lady Huntington, and wrote back,

> I thank your Ladyship for the information concerning these preachers. Their doctrines are most repulsive and strongly tinctured with impertinence and disrespect toward their superiors in that they are perpetually endeavoring to level all ranks and do away with all distinctions. It is monstrous to be told that you have a heart as sinful as the common lechers that crawl on the earth. This is highly offensive and insulting and I cannot but wonder that your Ladyship should relish any sentiment so much at variance with high rank and good breeding.[25]

Unconsciously, Lady Huntington was aiding the leveling process on two fronts: by recognizing the preachers of Methodism and by taking initiative as a woman in supporting a movement that was awakening thousands to the truth of the gospel and quickening church life in Great Britain. To her four homes in Chelsea, London, Brighton and Bath, she invited distinguished personalities like Horace Walpole, Lord Bolingbroke, Lord Chesterfield and David Hume to come and hear George Whitefield. For the bishops of the Church of England, she had a curtained alcove called "Nicodemus' Corner"—so they could listen without being seen.

Like many abbesses in the medieval period, Lady Huntington used her powerful position to promote the gospel of Jesus Christ. Her motive was her love for the Lord, about whom she wrote:

> God fills every void in my life. I have not one wish, one will, one desire, but in Him. . . . I have wondered and stood amazed that God should make conquest of all within me by love. . . . I am brought to less than nothing, broken in pieces like the potter's vessel. I long to leap into the flames to get rid of my sinful flesh, that every atom of these ashes might be separate, that neither time, place, nor person should stay God's spirit.[26]

When she lost two of her seven children in a smallpox epidemic, Lady Huntington prayed, "May He increase my faith, animate my heart with zeal for His glory, enlarge my sphere, and make me more faithful in the sphere in which I serve."[27] Three years later, she was widowed at the age of thirty-nine. But she was more determined than ever to use her time and money for the service of her lord. She was best known for supporting the Calvinistic wing of the revival, but she also worked for unity among all Christians. Because she was a channel of God's love, she was used to bring Wesley and Whitefield together after their doctrinal split. Later Lady Huntington, the two Wesleys and Whitefield formed the "Quadruple Alliance" to promote their Christian harmony.

When six students were expelled from Oxford University for holding Methodist meetings, Lady Huntington decided it was time to start a seminary, and she told Wesley of her plan. She proposed a free education for three years with food, lodging and a suit of clothing each year, after which the graduates could serve in the denomination of their choice. When the seminary opened in a twelfth-cen-

tury mansion in South Wales, she laid down the guidelines, probably the most valuable advice given to ministerial
students by any woman in history:

Two points I must lay down as the most indispensable
qualification for a minister of the everlasting Gospel.
The first is the invariable conviction that the Church of
Christ can have no establishment on earth, but that which
came down from Heaven on the Day of Pentecost. This is
the true Church of Christ under all denominations on
earth. It cannot continue to exist without faith, which is
the gift of God. Ordinances must be administered by
faith and received by faith. . . . The more scriptural and
simple your sermons and to the heart, the better. Apply
to facts, with the knowledge of evils in your heart. That
is the truth our Lord must bless. He can witness to nothing else, as He essentially and emphatically is truth itself.
. . . I write thus, hoping and believing that you have
counted the cost, and that you truly mean to devote yourself unreservedly to the Lord Jesus Christ.[28]

The most outstanding graduates of this school were sent to
Savannah to evangelize the American colonies. The rest of
the graduates preached all over England.

By the end of her life, Lady Huntington had sold her
jewels to sponsor chapels and had moved into such humble quarters that visitors were shocked at the change of lifestyle. Yet it is estimated that a hundred thousand persons
heard the gospel in the sixty chapels she sponsored.

What were the factors that made it possible for this
woman not only to proclaim the good news but to take leadership in promoting the spread of the gospel all over England and America? In the climate of revival, men and
women, rich and poor came to the cross and were accepted into the company of believers on the basis of grace
alone. In addition to this, the fact that Lady Huntington
was a member of the aristocracy also helped to overshadow

the fact that she was "only a woman." While it may take only a few women to break ground in men's territory, it takes thousands of women in each generation to maintain and cultivate the areas that have been won. Too often ground is lost, and the same battles have to be fought over again with each new generation.

# CHAPTER NINE

# Building Christianity in the New World: 1800-1900

THE SPIRIT OF THE WES-
leyan revival was imported to America by men like Henry
Worrall who had heard Wesley preach in England. In 1835,
his daughter Sarah started the "Tuesday Meeting for the
Promotion of Holiness" which continued every week for
over sixty years. Another daughter, Phoebe, also experienced renewal and said: "The Lord gave me such a view of
my utter pollution and helplessness, apart from the cleans-
ing, energizing influences of the purifying blood of Jesus,
and the quickening aids of the Holy Spirit, that I have ever
since retained a vivid realization of the fact."[1]

Phoebe Palmer is among that cloud of women witnesses
who had a first-love relationship with Jesus Christ. Because
she found her identity in that relationship, she had a deep
compulsion to introduce others to him. That's why she

wrote *Faith and Its Effects, The Way of Holiness* and *Present to My Christian Friend on Entire Devotion to God.* Later she became the editor of the *Guide to Holiness.*

Together with her physician husband who encouraged her and worked with her, Mrs. Palmer traveled up and down the East Coast and into Canada preaching. In 1857-58, she was a major force in the holiness revival which spread across the country. But she was not without opposition, and many churches closed their doors to her because she was a woman preacher. "The church in many ways is a sort of potter's field where the gifts of women, as so many strangers, are buried. How long, O Lord, how long before man shall roll away the stone that we may see a resurrection?" wrote Phoebe Palmer in *The Promise of the Father* (1859).[2] She decided to write this book after listening to a woman's anguish over having been called by God to speak publicly and then being reprimanded by the leaders of her church for wanting to obey.

### The Promise of the Father
Mrs. Palmer argues that the Father has poured his Spirit on his sons and daughters, expecting them to pray, preach and prophesy according to Joel 2:28-29. She also discusses the disorders in the church at Corinth in connection with Paul's prohibitions to women, and says,

It was in reference to this ... that Paul enjoins silence, and not in reference to the exercise of the gift of prophecy.... Surely it is evident that the irregularities here complained of were peculiar to the church of Corinth, and, in fact, we may presume, were not even applicable to other Christian churches of Paul's day, much less Christian churches of the present day, as no such disorders exist.[3]

Her book ends with the following call:

O, the endless weight of responsibility with which the

church is pressing herself earthward through the depressing influences of this error: How can she rise while the gifts of three-fourths of her membership are sepulchered in her midst?

Daughters of Zion, from the dust
Exalt thy fallen head;
Again in thy Redeemer trust.
He calls thee from the dead.[4]

## The Teachings of Finney

Even before Phoebe Palmer spoke out, Charles Finney had been encouraging women to pray and testify in public. Ordained by the Presbyterian Church in 1824, Finney became, according to V. Raymond Edman, "the most widely known and most successful American revivalist."[5]

Like Phoebe Palmer, Charles Finney had an everpresent sense of his own sin and constant gratitude to Jesus for all he had done. On one occasion Finney wrote: "it seemed as if my soul was wedded to Christ, in a sense in which I had never had any thought or conception of before. The language of the Song of Solomon was as natural to me as my breath. . . . I then realized what is meant by the saying He is able to do exceeding abundantly above all that we ask or think."[6]

Finney had to fight for the privilege of conducting "mixed meetings"—those including both men and women —and for letting women speak. He was charged with the great "evil to be apprehended . . . females praying in promiscuous [mixed] assemblies."[7] All the famous evangelists met to debate and settle this issue in 1827. Because Finney refused to compromise his stand, the door remained open for women to use their gifts in some of the churches that were touched by the revivals of the nineteenth century.

Joining Finney in the fight for these freedoms was abolitionist Theodore Weld, who had been converted in Finney's meeting in Utica, New York. Weld later wrote to Angelina and Sarah Grimki, both speakers for the cause of abolition:

> The very week that I was converted . . . and the first time I ever spoke in a religious meeting—I urged females both to pray and speak if they felt deeply enough to do it, and not to be restrained from it by the fact that they were females. . . . The result was that seven female Christians in the city confessed their sin in being restrained by their sex, and prayed publicly in succession at that very meeting.[8]

These women, who were sociologically conditioned not to pray in public, came to see their silence as a sin, where previously their attitudes were exactly the opposite.

Finney also encouraged Christian wives to speak to their unbelieving husbands about salvation. Such wives were often taught that the only verse applying to their situation is 1 Peter 3:1 where Peter suggests that sometimes husbands have to be won by the exemplary life of the wife without a word. Finney, however, suggested that wives have a responsibility to talk to their unbelieving husbands, but need to be guided by the Spirit in doing so: "I have known women who felt that they ought to talk to their unconverted husbands, and pray with them, but they have neglected it, and so they get into the dark. They knew their duty and refused to do it: they went around it, and there they lost the spirit of prayer."[9]

It is not surprising that many of the women who were touched by God in Finney's revivals became the feminist leaders of the nineteenth century. Elizabeth Cady Stanton was converted in Troy, New York. Caroline Severance was changed by revival in Auburn, and Antoinette Brown's father was converted in Rochester. Pauline Kellogg Wright Davis decided after Finney's revival near LeRoy that she wanted to be a missionary. Also, the first women's rights convention was held in a Wesleyan Methodist Church in Seneca Falls, New York, in 1848. Revival seemed to come hand in hand with concern for the rights of slaves and women.

The revivals also bought about the participation of lay people. In 1858 a "prayer meeting revival" swept across the nation with business people, farmers, factory workers and housewives gathering to sing hymns and to share testimonies. That year was referred to as the *annus mirabilis,* the extraordinary year. The Palmers were in Canada leading camp meetings, and the Finneys were in Boston. Charles Finney's second wife, Elizabeth Ford Atkinson, held meetings that "became so crowded, that the ladies would fill the room, and then stand about the door on the outside, as far as they could hear on every side."[10] In December of that year, the Finneys sailed for England where Elizabeth had spoken ten years earlier. Once again she had large crowds at all her meetings.

The Palmers went to England in June 1859, and there Phoebe Palmer profoundly influenced Catherine Mumford Booth, a young pastor's wife who later helped found the Salvation Army. After returning to the U.S., the Palmers traveled westward to hold meetings in Evanston, Illinois.

In Evanston, Frances Willard, who had just raised $30,000 to build the first hall of Garrett Bible Institute, attended a service. Willard, who had been converted through Finney's revivals, responded to Palmer's altar call for those who wanted the "higher Christian life." Ten years later, Willard received another call to become involved in the suffrage movement. At that time suffrage was considered "too advanced and radical a thing, connected in those days with too much ridicule and scorn, a thing unwomanly and unscriptural."[11] But Willard reported:

While alone on my knees one Sabbath, as I lifted my

heart to God crying, "What wouldst thou have me to do?" there was born in my mind, as I believe from loftier regions, this declaration. "You are to speak for woman's ballot as a weapon for protection for her home." Then for the first and only time in my life, there flashed through my brain a complete line of arguments and illustrations.[12] At first, the Women's Christian Temperance Union refused to let Frances Willard speak on suffrage. But after she became the WCTU national president, she used the organization as the training ground for women who later became leaders in the National American Women's Suffrage Association. One of these was Anna Howard Shaw, who was both a medical doctor and an ordained Methodist Protestant minister and who worked with both the WCTU and the National American Women's Suffrage Association from 1888 to 1915. Another was Hannah Whitall Smith, prominent leader in the holiness movement who is best known for her book *The Christian's Secret of a Happy Life* She and her husband were active in founding the English Keswick movement.

### Amanda Smith and the Holiness Movement

Evangelist Amanda Smith was another woman who combined the holiness movement with the freedom to speak as a woman. Born a slave, she challenged people's prejudice against blacks and women. When she experienced God's renewal at a meeting in 1868, she wanted to shout, "Glory to Jesus!" But, as she remarked later, "I was the only colored person there and I had a very keen sense of propriety." By the end of the meeting, however, God had delivered her from her fear of white people by reminding her of Galatians 3:28: "There is neither Jew nor Greek, slave nor free, male nor female, for you are all one in Christ Jesus."

As she began attending holiness camp meetings, testifying and singing, she recalls: "The Lord cured a good old brother, Jacob C., of prejudice. . . . When he saw me about in the meetings he was much disturbed. But still he felt he needed the blessing, and had come to camp meeting for that purpose. Whenever the invitation was given for those who wanted a clean heart, he would go forward and kneel down." But then when the black woman sang, prayed or testified, he was blocked and could not go on. He finally had to get out into the woods and pray alone before he was able to "make a full surrender of himself."[13]

At a national meeting in Knoxville, Tennessee, Amanda Smith gave her testimony and a Methodist minister who had been a staunch opponent of holiness began to weep. He stepped onto the platform and confessed his sin of prejudice against the doctrine of holiness, adding: "When I heard this colored sister tell how God had led her and brought her into this blessed experience, the darkness swept away and God has saved me, and I see the truth as I never did before. Glory to God!"[14]

Amanda Smith was thus used of God to break down prejudice on three fronts: against the doctrine of holiness, against blacks, and against female evangelists. Her missionary journeys took her to Keswick, England, to Africa for a number of years, and to India. There Bishop Thoburn observed, "She possessed a clearness of vision which I have found seldom equalled. . . . During the seventeen years that I lived in Calcutta, I have known many famous strangers to visit the city, but I have never known anyone who could draw and hold so large an audience as Mrs. Smith."[15]

The holiness denominations that grew out of the revivals of Smith's time continued to give women opportunities to preach. The Church of God, founded in 1881, published its *Familiar Names and Faces* in 1902. Fifty of the two hundred leaders mentioned were women. And the Church of the Nazarene did not even debate whether women should preach. Historian Timothy Smith writes about women preachers, including his mother:

> The women who carried on this independent gospel work seem to have combined piety and practicality to a remarkable degree. Between revivals they maintained a normal and apparently stable family life, if the few surviving letters may be taken at face value. Their husbands joined happily in their meetings when they were near home and accepted periods of separation without much protest.[16]

Women had similar experiences in the Pilgrim Holiness Church, founded in 1897 with Seth Cook Rees as its president. The father of Paul S. Rees, a director of World Vision International, Seth Rees wrote:

> Nothing but jealousy, prejudice, bigotry, and a stingy love for bossing in men have prevented woman's public recognition by the church. No church that is acquainted with the Holy Ghost will object to the public ministry of women. We know scores of women who can preach the Gospel with a clearness, a power, and an efficiency seldom equalled by men. Sisters, let the Holy Ghost fill, call and anoint you to preach the glorious Gospel of our Lord.[17]

Rees's wife, Hulda, was known as the "Pentecostal prophetess," having preached since she was sixteen. She accompanied her husband as copastor and coevangelist. Her stepson, Paul S. Rees, said of her, "Like Catherine Booth, she was a balanced soul in whom domestic virtues and platform gifts developed apace."[18]

Not every woman in the holiness movement became a preacher like Hulda Rees, but all were encouraged to testify publicly. Historian Melvin Dieter writes, "It was the theology of the (Holiness) movement and the essential nature of the place of public testimony in the holiness experience which gave many an otherwise timid woman the authority and the power to speak out 'as the Holy Spirit led her.' . . . To those who allowed the theology, the logic was irrefutable."[19]

Because of this emphasis on declaring what God has done, silence became almost a sin, as Phoebe Upham suggests: "To *impart* what one receives from God is the out-going life of the new Christ-nature. . . . How opposed then to the new Christ-nature, and to God's Word, is the sealing of woman's lips in the public exercises of the Church."[20]

Writing on the same subject in the *Guide to Holiness*, Sadie Hart, a Presbyterian, said that her refusal to pray in public was "the one step between me and the kingdom." She denied the right of women to pray at prayer meetings until a Methodist elder gave her a "talking to." After confessing her prejudice, she was open to God's blessing in her life.[21]

A minister's wife from a similar background came out of her cocoon in one of Phoebe Palmer's meetings. She "was changed from a timid, shrinking, silent Christian, into one of tearful, modest, but pentecostal power, and who afterwards spoke in public, with remarkable effect."[22]

Like Palmer many women quoted Joel's prophecy, cited by Peter in Acts 2:17-18, as the basis for women proclaiming God's Word. Among them, Jennie Fowler Willing, a licensed Methodist preacher, called Pentecost "Woman's Emancipation Day" and declared that "Pentecost laid the axe at the root of the tree of social injustice."[23] Pentecost was looked on as the beginning of a new age, which offered a widened ministry for women as the sign of the outpouring of God's Spirit before Christ's Second Coming. Preaching was not looked on as the result of human effort or training, but as the influence of the Holy Spirit. Often the nonprofessional preacher would use a style of preaching called "Bible readings." The speaker would read a passage and make appropriate comments under the guidance of the Holy Spirit.

The Holy Spirit was always emphasized in the holiness movement. First, Wesley had spoken of the Spirit's witnessing to the believer's sanctification. Later, sanctification was equated with the baptism of the Holy Spirit. This was Charles Finney's emphasis. Because Pentecost was central to the experience of holiness, believers expected extraordinary gifts. With a charismatic concept of ministry instead of a hierarchical one, the cultural differences between men and women were more easily set aside. The gifts were given to men and women alike, and all were leveled at the cross.

But while this holiness emphasis continued into the twentieth century, the radical egalitarianism of pre-Civil War days was lost. The struggle for women to proclaim the gospel could no longer go hand in hand with the struggle for the rights of slaves for their freedom, because after the Civil War there was a tendency to look on the abolitionist aims as accomplished.

Another factor in the loss of the nineteenth-century gains for women was the change from charismatic leadership to professionalized leadership and organized church institutions. For instance, in many of the Bible schools and colleges founded in the nineteenth century, a number of faculty members in the English, theology and Bible departments were women. But as these schools became full-fledged colleges, many of the women lacked the required academic degrees. In the ministry, women faced the same problem, as churches began demanding seminary-trained pastors. "In the 1930's to 1950's daughters did not follow in the footsteps of their preacher and professorial mothers and grandmothers; thus these role models were lost for the present generation to rediscover."[24]

Although the holiness movement, which covered two

hundred years from the time of the Wesleys and Whitefield until the first part of the twentieth century, had a very major influence on women, there were other movements which also made a difference.

### The Scandinavian Revivals and the Free Churches

The movements that came out of the Scandinavian revivals of the nineteenth century also played a significant part in shaping women's role. A friend explained to me how he was converted to Jesus Christ: "It was up on the Iron Range during special meetings with a Swedish Baptist woman evangelist." I have since discovered that the Swedish Baptists, now known as the Baptist General Conference, have a great heritage of women preachers. As recently as World War 2, Ethel Ruff was ordained in Payne Avenue Baptist Church in St. Paul, Minnesota.[25]

Fredrik Franson was a Swedish missionary strategist who had a significant impact on Scandinavian Christians in the last part of the nineteenth century, especially in the area of women preaching the gospel. One of the churches that Franson was influential in starting was the Evangelical Free Church.

In 1888, in one of the earliest annual conferences of this denomination, one item to be discussed read, "Does God's Word permit a woman to preach, participate in all Christian work and have the right to a voice in the decisions of the congregation?"[26] The discussion that followed appeared in the Swedish-language newspaper *Chicago Bladet* and included the following contribution:

> Acts 21:9 states that the evangelist Philip had four daughters who prophesied and it even says they were unmarried. The word "prophesy" is from Greek and "preach" from Latin but they mean the same. In order to prophesy or preach one must be before an assembly not just with one person; otherwise it would be convers-

ing. If it was acceptable for a woman to preach in those days it should also be so in our time. When we see how God is blessing believing sisters such as Nelly Hall to the salvation of many souls, and the strengthening of God's children this should be convincing evidence. There has been no schism in any congregation following her ministry. Should any come it would be through unwise individuals who give themselves to disputing about whether or not it is right for a woman to preach; but for this she would not be responsible. God is with her and she speaks, anointed by the Holy Spirit, while many preachers are so dry they creak.[27]

The urgency about getting the gospel proclaimed is heard in another comment made by a man at the same conference in 1888: "May the spirit of muteness flee from both men and women for it is dreadful how silent we have become about the Lord and His grace both in our homes and at social gatherings as well as in the circle of fellowship. Where two or three are gathered in His Name that is the fellowship of believers."[28]

After another free-church conference in Chicago in 1896, churches in each area were encouraged to form associations. Della Olson writes about the Joliet conference that resulted in an association of preachers, evangelists, elders and Sunday-school superintendents among Swedish, Norwegian and Danish free-church believers in Illinois and adjacent states. These churches eventually became Evangelical Free churches. She goes on to tell that when the bylaws of the association were written, women were mentioned in three of them. The first one reads: "The association has not considered itself justified in denying membership to women evangelists who have been called to that work by a local congregation."[29]

Yet in 1978 in that same area a young woman attended the Thanksgiving service in an Evangelical Free church.

When she arrived at the table where we were celebrating Thanksgiving together, she was upset. The minister that morning had asked only for the men of the church to share how God had blessed them in the past year.

Today, within the Evangelical Free church, opportunities for women to speak are much more limited. Della Olson, however, has chronicled the active role that women took in the churches in the nineteenth and early twentieth century. In *A Woman of Her Times* she gives women this challenge: "There are still the conventional, accepted roles—singing in the choir, participating in all kinds of children's work, being involved in the Women's Missionary Society, and, of course, serving church dinners and coffee hours. But is that all there is? Surely not for Free Church women, who would continue in the train of those who were 'women of their time.' "[30]

Yet the vision that free-church women had has largely been lost. Shortly before World War 2, according to Donald Dayton, the evangelical church began to conform to the thinking of the secular world with regard to women.[31] The virile evangelicalism that fought injustices in the name of the Lord was replaced by a preoccupation with correct doctrine and rules about do's and don'ts. The age of revival was gone, and with a return to "business as usual," the old prejudices against women began to surface.

Then came World War 2 with many women having to do "men's work" while sons, husbands and fathers fought for their country. War-weary, the men came back with a desire for women to return to housekeeping and childrearing. The feminine mystique was the philosophy of womanhood that developed out of society's longing to go back to the "good ol' days."

But are the "good ol' days" necessarily good? While the Christians failed to ask or answer this question, the secular world raised its own questions about women's roles during the turbulent sixties. With very little input from the church, the answers to these questions became the basis of a left-wing radical feminism that has disturbed Christians and humanists alike.

Just as the feminine mystique was a reaction against the war years, so the backlash against women's liberation was society's way of reacting against the unknown changes that feminism might bring. With the tension between the two sides, evangelical Christians found themselves trapped in a corner between two bad choices. Should they join the radical feminists or the antifeminists? Many did not realize that both groups were inspired by human culture, not Christianity.

Many evangelicals have tended to join the antifeminists. But as such evangelical women are defensive rather than offensive for Jesus Christ. The opportunity for women to present the gospel as a positive, liberating force for good has often been neutralized in the heat of battle. We wonder what has happened to the preaching of the cross in our day. And what has happened to the tradition of brave women throughout the ages who have preached Christ crucified and been willing to die for the One who is their first love?

The call to enter the kingdom through Jesus, the Way, needs to be proclaimed by both men and women. We have a world to win for Jesus Christ. The ship is sinking, and we are standing on the shore arguing about who should go to the rescue—men or women. Whether we are men or women, we have the opportunity to proclaim the gospel "publicly and from house to house" (Acts 20:20). What a privilege that God wants us involved! There is intimacy and joy in following Jesus, the fierce joy of being loyal to the One who is our first love.

Jesus Christ offered such joy to the small band of women who followed him. As he gave them their special commission, he was speaking to women throughout the ages: "Go quickly and tell . . . : 'He has risen from the dead' " (Mt 28: 7). Did they protest that they were just women? No. Motivated by love, they were willing to take risks in proclaiming the good news.

# PART FOUR

# Jesus Christ
# in All of Life

# CHAPTER TEN

# Ministering as Single Women

**B**UT WHAT IF I BECOME an old maid?" the sweet, softspoken blonde blurted out, looking like an angel with sparkling puddles around her bright blue eyes. Slowly I watched the pretty face wrinkle up and get soaked with salty tears. This was no minor tragedy for Cindy. She felt her whole neat world had been shaken by an earthquake. And I was shaken too—too shaken to be of much help.

This scene took place while Bob and I were in a U.S. pastorate years ago. Cindy had asked to talk to us about her "hardheaded" parents who forbade her to date a boy who was not a Christian. She poured out her heart about how few Christian boys there were in town and asked in exasperation, "What chances are there for me here?" In Cindy's mind, nothing worse could happen to her than to be an old maid. She was thirteen.

Her words shocked me. My last overseas post had been
with Asian women, many of whom went against their patriarchal culture and begged their fathers—also with tears
—to let them stay single a little longer, so they could serve
only Jesus Christ.

Obviously, it was unfair to compare Cindy with those
dedicated young women from a culture where parents
helped their daughters find husbands. Cindy was brought
up in a community that made it difficult for her to see that
Christ could satisfy the deepest longings of her inner being
(Ps 107:9).

In another setting, not too long before I met Cindy, I
was stunned when a godly woman whom I admired said,
"It seems like the single gals are God's stepchildren." Does
God have favorite children—and less favorite ones? Are
there second-class Christians in the family of God?

If God has no favorites, then the single Christian woman
is given complete fulfillment in Jesus Christ as she sits at
Jesus' feet and then passes on to others what she has learned.
The woman of God needs neither sexual fulfillment nor
male protection, neither husband nor children to give her
a place in church and society and a sense of identity as a
person. She can find fulfillment in the creative expression
of her sexuality as a woman.

To her is given the beautiful opportunity that Paul pre-
sents: "An unmarried woman . . . is concerned about the
Lord's affairs: Her aim is to be devoted to the Lord in both
body and spirit. But a married woman is concerned about
the affairs of this world—how she can please her husband.
I am saying this for your own good, not to restrict you, but
that you may live in a right way in undivided devotion to the
Lord. . . . A woman is bound to her husband as long as he
lives. But if her husband dies, she is free to marry anyone
she wishes, but he must belong to the Lord. In my judgment, she is happier if she stays as she is—and I think that

I too have the Spirit of God" (1 Cor 7:34-35, 39-40).

Few passages in the New Testament have been more ignored. The same Christians who interpret Paul literally at other points sometimes overlook these strong words favoring the single life for believers in Corinth: "Now about virgins: I have no command from the Lord, but I give a judgment as one who by the Lord's mercy is trustworthy. *Because of the present crisis,* I think that it is good for you to remain as you are.... But if you do marry, you have not sinned; and if a virgin marries, she has not sinned. But those who marry will face many troubles in this life, and I want to spare you this. What I mean ... is that the time is short. From now on those who have wives should live as if they had none; ... those who use the things of the world, as if not engrossed in them. For this world in its present form is passing away. I would like you to be free from concern" (1 Cor 7:25-26, 28-32, my emphasis).

We get a glimpse here of singleness in the light of eternal values. In the pages ahead we will contrast God's attitude with that of human beings toward the single woman. We will begin with a look into the Old Testament.

**The Genesis Account**

Whether women consider themselves as being single by choice or by circumstance, God's attitude toward them is of primary importance. Almost all women in all cultures are single during some years of their adult lives, and numerous women between the ages of eighteen and seventy-eight are single for more years than they are married. How many women do you know who have been married thirty, forty, fifty or sixty years? Scanzoni and Hardesty report in *All We're Meant to Be* that in 1974 there were 16.5 million unmarried women over twenty-five in the United States. Of these, 4.2 million had never been married, while the rest had been separated, widowed or divorced.[1]

If single women are not God's stepchildren, then a loving Creator must have some beautiful reason for allowing
them to be single all of their lives or most of it. First, God's
loving attitude is revealed in the very first chapter of the
Bible. We might assume that God created because he
wanted companions—persons who would reflect the image
of God and so could communicate with their Creator. Since
we were created for God, our natural response becomes
one of adoration and love expressed through worship to
the One who "created man in his own image, in the image of
God he created him; male and female he created them"
(Gen 1:27).

God's image included male and female, and there is no
mention of marriage here. The specific instructions for
male and female follow: be fruitful and multiply, subdue
the earth, and have dominion over every living thing. Of
the three assignments, we seem to have accomplished only
the first. Since we now have a population explosion, single
women can relax. But we haven't yet subdued the earth
or taken dominion over our natural resources. We haven't
discovered all possible means of food production. People
are still starving. Two jobs remain unfinished and need
the cooperation of all women and men so that humanity
can enjoy the divine dignity God originally intended for
us as reflections of the divine image.

God's intention was not to produce a conflict of interest
between people. He did not divide them into rich and poor
or more-favored and less-favored nations. And certainly
there was no implication in this first story of inequality between the sexes. Rather there is the suggestion of a com-
plementary relationship between male and female that
transcends the marriage relationship. That is why Paul felt
so strongly that in Christ there is no male or female (Gal
3:28). Intuitively, he knew that the old order was wrong
where only men could form a quorum to make up a syna-

gogue. He was beginning to see how male and female together represent the unity of the Godhead with its three parts.

When we make single women feel that they are misfits in the church, we have failed to accept them as part of the image of God, and thus failed to respond to God's first lesson about male and female equality. Augustine missed the mark in this respect when he wrote, "The woman herself alone is not the image of God: whereas the man alone is the image of God as fully and completely as when the woman is joined with him."[2] Little did the great saint know that he was adding to the persecution of women—especially single women—for ages to come. Because he was blinded, he also failed to realize that by persecuting someone in God's image, he was persecuting God.

This truth was clearly illustrated after Saul "began to destroy the church. Going from house to house, he dragged off men and women and put them in prison." Later, when Saul was accosted on the road to Damascus, the Voice asked, "Saul, Saul, why do you persecute *me?*" (Acts 8:3; 9:4, italics added). The implication is that Saul was persecuting Jesus when he put those men and women in prison. And today we are doing likewise when we discriminate against single women who are created in God's image. We can hear the same Voice saying, "I am Jesus, whom you are persecuting" (Acts 9:5).

### According to Luke

The only perfect man who never discriminated against single women was Jesus Christ. Precisely because the Savior was single, he could understand what single people had to face in a society where marriage was the norm. In fact, in the Gospels we have more references to women independent of their marital status than to women within the context of their roles as wives. This may come as a surprise to us in an age when the church has become so family centered that it tends to exclude singles. As I was encouraging a widowed friend to go to the church that her son and his family attended, she retorted, "Oh, churches don't want old ladies like me. They like young couples with children."

By contrast, the writings of Luke in his Gospel and in Acts come to us as good news for the single woman. In Luke 1 we are introduced to Mary, a virgin, who through an angelic visit received her "Great Commission" from God. In Luke 2 we meet Anna, a woman of eighty-four who had been widowed after only seven years of marriage and then lived in the temple as a prophet. Jesus speaks of another widow in Luke 4 who fed Elijah during a famine, and he raises the son of the widow of Nain in Luke 7. He commends the sinful woman who anointed his feet with perfume: "Her many sins have been forgiven—for she loved much" (Lk 7:47).

Luke 8 starts with the list of women "who had been cured of evil spirits and diseases" and traveled with Jesus, paying the bills for the team at inns and eating places. Only Joanna is identified as the wife of someone. How many of the rest were single? We can only guess that some were divorced because they found no favor in their husbands' eyes due to "some uncleanness" (see Deut 24:1 KJV). These women must have been thrilled to hear that they, along with all "those who hear God's word and put it into practice," are Jesus' mother (Lk 8:21). What good news for single women.

The chapter ends with the story of the woman "who had been subject to bleeding for twelve years" (Lk 8:43). She was unclean all the time and made anyone she touched unclean (Lev 15:19-33). Somehow she trusted Jesus enough to touch him; she was restored and was called to give public testimony of her healing.

In Luke 10, Jesus visits two single women with whom he had a unique friendship (see also Jn 11). Martha trusts him enough to complain about having to do all the house-work! We have mentioned earlier how Jesus loves them both, but points out that Mary has chosen the superior role —that of the disciple, "and it will not be taken away from her."

But it has been taken away from many women who have tried to follow in Mary's footsteps. Margaret Clarkson, a single woman who is a poet and teacher, writes, "Whatever her ability, experience, or spiritual gifts, a woman is usually expected to fill a traditional female role in the church, likely in the kitchen or with babies or young children. She may not be especially suited to this, and other work which she could do better may be crying out for workers; but no matter."[3]

In the time of Jesus, after a disciple like Mary had sat at the feet of a master, he or she would be expected to pass on to others what had been learned. What about godly women today who have sat at Jesus' feet for years and have so much to pass on, yet are never given the opportunity?

Maybe Jesus had such women in mind when he announced in Luke 11 that he did not think of women only in their reproductive role—as giving birth and nursing babies. What good news for childless women to hear: "Blessed rather are those who hear the word of God and obey it" (11:28). By contrast, one single woman with a Ph.D. in English and a job as professor in a local college told me that she feels out of place in church because "I have not added to the species, which in turn would add new members to the Sunday School." Has biological growth become more important to us than reaching those who have never heard the gospel? And has biology become the destiny for Christian women rather than spiritual commitment to Jesus Christ?

Jesus returns to this subject when the Sadducees ask him about the woman who was married to seven brothers and failed to produce children in all seven marriages. Who would be her husband in the resurrection? The question was a test of Jesus' view of the resurrection. But his answer is also important to women today. Jesus replied, "The people of this age marry and are given in marriage. But those who are considered worthy of taking part in that age and in the resurrection from the dead will neither marry nor be given in marriage, and they can no longer die; for they are like the angels. They are God's children, since they are children of the resurrection" (20:34-39). Jesus sees women as children of God, not wives of husbands.

Luke goes on in chapters 18 and 21 to relate two of Jesus' stories about widows—one who was an illustration of persistence, used in Jesus' talk on prayer, and another who was a model of generosity when she gave all she had to God (18:1-8; 21:1-4). The Gospel writer winds up his account by returning to the women of Galilee who followed Jesus to Jerusalem to be present at his trial, death, burial and resurrection (chap. 24). Luke starts his story in Acts with some of the same women present in the upper room (Acts 1:13-14), waiting for the gift from the Father.

While Mary Magdalene, whom most authorities regard as a single woman, was the first announcer to the disciples that Jesus Christ had risen from the dead, another single woman became a heroine as the first convert on the European continent. In Philippi the women met for prayer. We have already mentioned how Lydia was the first to respond to Paul's message and open her home for Christian worship (Acts 16:14).

God also sent Peter to raise Dorcas from the dead. Probably a widow surrounded by other widows, Dorcas sewed garments for the poor (Acts 9:36-41). Meanwhile, over in Caesarea, "Philip the evangelist, one of the Seven... had four unmarried daughters who had the gift of prophecy" (Acts 21:8-9).

## Single Women in World Mission

The great tradition of "prophesying daughters" has continued from the time of Pentecost. Single women have been among the pioneers in the modern missionary movement. As early as 1882, missionary societies started for women had sent out and supported 694 unmarried women in world mission.[4] The same year, the China Inland Mission had 56 wives and 95 single women in China. And already in 1888, Hudson Taylor, the founder of the C.I.M., reported that many stations in inland China were being "manned" by single women.[5]

By 1900, according to R. Pierce Beaver, dean of American missiologists, there were 1,015 single women missionaries sent out from the United States. This number more than doubled to 2,122 in 1910, and redoubled to 4,824 in 1923.[6] Meanwhile, William Lennox, reporting on six U.S. mission boards in *The Health and Turnover of Missionaries,* wrote: "In 1830, like animals entering the Ark, missionaries went to the field in pairs. . . . [But] the missionary personnel was female to the extent of 49% in 1830, 57% in 1880, and 67% in 1929."[7]

Much of the encouragement for single women to enter missionary service came from mission boards that were founded to help women fulfill the Great Commission of our Lord. Helen Montgomery, best known for her translation of the Bible, said that there were forty-four organized missionary societies for women in 1910, supported by two million women who raised four million dollars in one year.[8] According to Ralph Winter of the U.S. Center for World Mission, all of these have been discontinued. Winter says that the first women's society was formed in 1865 and dissolved in 1980. This society, which was Methodist, was also the largest such society on record.[9]

The resulting decline of single women in missions shows up in the statistics of the *Mission Handbook: North American*

*Protestant Ministries Overseas.* For 1976 they show a grand total of 31,186 career missionaries, of whom 4,643 are single women. Only 59.96% of the total missionary force today are women in contrast to Lennox's figure of 67% in 1929.[10]

As Beaver tries to account for the decline of single women in world mission, he mentions as one reason "the present social pressure for a girl to marry young," but adds that "the most potent factor has been the termination of a distinctive women's missionary movement carried out through women's agencies." He goes on to say, "The greatest loss consequent to the end of the distinctive organized women's world mission movement has been the decline of missionary dynamism and zeal in the churches. . . . Never since the decade of 1810 and 1820 has commitment to world mission been so low in our Protestant churches . . . in large measure due to the decline of women's direct participation."[11]

With the secularization of society and the church, what are the prospects of reviving women's missionary agencies so that the single woman can again find that special place of service where she can express her first love for Jesus Christ? In many parts of the world, I have met single women who are ready to give themselves to the concerns that are on the Savior's heart if they can just find the right group to work with.

Mother Teresa of Calcutta is one such woman. She is probably the best-known single woman missionary in the world today. Malcolm Muggeridge has given her and her Missionaries of Charity the most beautiful tribute:

Their life is tough and austere by worldly standards, certainly: yet I never met such delightful, happy women, or such an atmosphere of joy as they create. Mother Teresa, as she is fond of explaining, attaches the utmost importance to this joyousness. The poor, she says, deserve not just service and dedication, but also the joy that belongs to human love.... The Missionaries of Charity... are multiplying at a fantastic rate. Their Calcutta house is bursting at the seams, and as each new house is opened, there are volunteers clamouring to go there. As the whole story of Christendom shows, if everything is asked for, everything—and more—will be accorded; if little, then nothing.[12]

Muggeridge's reaction to the Calcutta sisters reminds me of a similar experience I had. Travel-weary and satiated with sightseeing in Europe, we arrived at the Sisters of Mary in Darmstadt, Germany, an order with a Lutheran orientation. Joy was written on the faces of the sisters. We had entered a bit of Canaan where the atmosphere was charged with the presence of the Almighty. And from Darmstadt these sisters have fanned out around the world. We found among them a mix of widows and virgins, much like the Order of Widows and Virgins John Chrysostom wrote about (when he reported there were three thousand sisters in the church of Antioch alone).[13] Perhaps it is time to return to the concept of orders for single women to give them that special place they need to function for Jesus Christ effectively in the church and in the mission of the church around the world.

## The Advantages of Singleness

In spite of the overwhelming evidence that God uses single women in the mission of the church, one Christian writing a book on marriage says, "The plan of the Creator is marriage, not singleness.... The plan of God is marriage. Singleness for religious service is a cultural tradition and not the plan of God."[14] Others are not quite so blunt but, as Scanzoni and Hardesty point out, "Ministers are notorious for their cruel 'jokes' about single women missionaries."[15]

Certainly the teaching of Jesus does not support such a

narrow view. After the disciples had heard Jesus' words on divorce, they responded, "If this is the situation between a husband and wife, it is better not to marry" (Mt 19:10). Jesus gave the classic reply, "Not everyone can accept this teaching, but only those to whom it has been given. For some are eunuchs because they were born that way; others were made that way by men; and others have renounced marriage because of the kingdom of heaven. The one who can accept this should accept it" (vv. 11-12).

The Savior is telling us here that the single life is not for all. Our mistake today is to think it is not for anyone. Jesus is very practical and explains that there are different kinds of people and needs. He also upholds the high calling of giving up, for the sake of the kingdom of God, not one's sexuality but the physical expression of sex.

Some Christians do not pay any attention to this teaching of Jesus, nor to Paul's on the same subject. They teach, directly or indirectly, that no celibate human being can find fulfillment. This is a sign of the church being conformed to the world's standards. We get our values from TV shows and movies which stimulate the sexual appetite to demand satisfaction. Our society expects everyone "naturally" to engage in sexual experience or fantasy, and the contemplation of giving up sex for a higher good is nearly unthinkable. Contrast with this Jesus' teaching on lust in Matthew 5:27-28.

Squeezed into the sex-crazy world's mold, Christian young people rush into marriage. "You can't live without sex" is the premise. The church accepts this and adds, "Christians can only have sex in marriage." Therefore the young Christian concludes, "I'd better hurry up and find a mate."

Sex is not the only drive within us. We also have a drive to succeed, an urge to develop our abilities and use them for God's glory. Middle-aged women often look back on lost opportunities to become all that God intended them to be. Among these women, a number have admitted that they would have been far better off if they had remained single and found their fulfillment in creative activity as an alternate expression of their sexuality. Others have confessed with tears that as teen-agers they dedicated their lives to God's service. But instead of considering marriage only if they met a man for whom Jesus Christ also came first, they left their first love for the love of a mere human being.

Just as many regret their marriages today, Paul must have known many in his day who envied him for being single. And yet Paul's concern in 1 Corinthians 7 is not singleness for its own sake, but putting the Lord Jesus Christ ahead of all other interests. He sees the practical difficulty of trying to put Christ first in marriage, and so suggests it is better to remain single. The reason he gives is "because of the present crisis." Do we have a similar crisis today? Is America like Corinth? We all know of modern marriages that have been shattered. Our times are also like Noah's. Jesus warns us, "Just as it was in the days of Noah, so also will it be in the days of the Son of Man. People were eating, drinking, marrying and being given in marriage up to the day Noah entered the ark. Then the flood came and destroyed them all" (Lk 17:26-27).

Sometimes the very young are the most sensitive to the times in which we live. I was deeply moved when a ten-year-old boy in our church told his mother, "I don't think I'll have a family. I think I just need to be busy for Jesus."

But what about our human need for love, for touch, for community? Remember, Jesus suggested that within the Christian family we can find our mothers, brothers and sisters (Mk 3:31-35). No single woman should live alone, isolated from other Christians. She needs the companionship of both men and women. That's why Christian communities are being formed today.[16] At times of loneliness and temptation, the single woman needs someone to hold her up, for "two are better than one.... If one falls down, her friend can help her up. But pity the woman who falls and has no one to help her up!... Though one may be overpowered, two can defend themselves. A cord of three strands is not quickly broken" (Eccles 4:9-10, 12, my changes).

The mention of two or three helping each other reminds us of the perfect fellowship of two or three who pray together (Mt 18:19-20). Within the context of such fellowship, the single woman will receive and give help. Sometimes she will use her God-given instinct for mothering. Parental instincts need not be wasted in single women and men. Paul used such instincts in his relationships to the churches. Paul compares himself to a mother in Galatians 4:19 and 1 Thessalonians 2:7. And Jesus calls himself a "mother hen" in Matthew 23:37.

The world is full of lost people, motherless children and fragmented families who need our help. We can all participate in mothering, caring and nurturing. In such a way we fulfill our basic need to be needed, to reproduce ourselves in another by loving that person into the kingdom.

The motivating force behind all such acts of love is the single woman's relationship with Jesus Christ. While human love for all of us might be here today and gone tomorrow, the divine Lover is always there, full of promises of love:

"Sing, O barren woman,
   you who never bore a child;
burst into song, shout for joy,
   you who were never in labor;
because more are the children of the desolate woman
   than of her who has a husband....

For your Maker is your husband—

the LORD Almighty is his name—
the Holy One of Israel is your Redeemer;
he is called the God of all the earth. . . .

Though the mountains be shaken
and the hills be removed,
yet my unfailing love for you will not be shaken
nor my covenant of peace be removed,"
says the LORD, who has compassion on you.
(Is 54:1, 5,10)

Fulfillment outside marriage—is it possible for the Christian woman? To doubt it would be to doubt God's promises.

# CHAPTER ELEVEN

# Interacting as Married Women

IMAGINE THE TEMPERA-
ture and humidity soaring hand in hand into the steaming
nineties—spring, summer, fall and winter. We were living
in the south of the Philippines, a few degrees of latitude
from the equator, in a land where people seldom discussed
the heat that varied little from day to day. This made for-
eigners easy to spot with their preoccupation with slight
temperature changes and perspiration problems.

My husband—bent on adjusting to the customs of the
land—determined not to be caught discussing the weather.
He wouldn't even write home about it! But since I handled
the correspondence with the churches that backed our
mission project, I managed to sneak in a weather report
now and then. Bob, checking one of these letters, cast a
strong veto: "But you talked about the weather last time.

You're really overdoing this; you're complaining—sounding like you want sympathy."

I was miffed. Since I was bearing the burden of communicating with the churches, I felt I should have some "freedom of the press." However, I also wanted harmony with my husband and so grudgingly erased the weather report.

About three weeks later a package arrived from one of the churches that had been receiving our letters. First Church had all sorts of surprises for us. And for the children—so their little hands would not get cold in that far-away land—lovely woolen mittens! Score one for me.

The conflict between the sexes sometimes appears in clownish costume, and we can all have a good laugh about it. At other times it becomes a game of one-upmanship. The marriage partners may even keep score on how often each one has been proven right. Sometimes the battle turns into a game of chance. Circumstances seem to cooperate in favor of one of the partners. One is the winner, the other a loser.

For those who get tired of the contest, the score is often settled in a divorce court. We can hear Jesus protesting: "Moses permitted you to divorce your wives because your hearts were hard. But it was not this way from the beginning.... Haven't you read ... that at the beginning the Creator 'made them male and female,' and said, 'For this reason a man will leave his father and mother and be united to his wife, and the two will become one flesh'? So they are no longer two, but one. Therefore what God has joined together, let man not separate" (Mt 19:8, 4-6).

What is God suggesting? Because a man and woman are related to the great God who created them, they can expect the *agape* love that exists between the Creator and the created ones to exist also between two humans who are united in marriage, so that no third party or problem can separate them.

Does this sound like an impossible model to our modern ears? All through history, men and women have questioned the basic assumption that God joins two human lives in a love knot that is strong enough to hold. To examine the paradox of what marriage was intended to be and what it has become, we shall look first at the first perfect marriage.

## Paradise

After the creation of male and female in Genesis 1, we have a more detailed account of how Adam and Eve were created in Genesis 2. First we read that "the Lord God formed man from the dust of the ground and breathed into his nostrils the breath of life" (v. 7). The breath of God is in mankind because humans have been created in the image of God. As such, "man" (in the generic sense) has the privilege of communicating with God—to love, worship, praise, and adore the Creator. This distinguishes humans from animals. We are created to "glorify God and to enjoy Him forever" (Westminster Catechism).

Next, the distinction between the sexes is introduced by God saying, "It is not good for the man to be alone. I will make a helper suitable for him" (v. 18). God intends humans to live in fellowship, not in solitude. There is the suggestion here that solitude leads to helplessness. By contrast, a companion will be a helper. Paul Jewett of Fuller Theological Seminary comments on humanity as "shared humanity (Mitmenschlichkeit). Humanity that is not shared humanity is inhumanity. . . . Shared humanity is what it is because Man is like God."[1]

So what kind of helper did God create to introduce Adam to the "I and thou" relationship? The Hebrew word *ezer* (translated "helper"), according to Berkeley and Alvera Mickelsen, does not imply subordination. It is used in other cases to describe God as our "helper" (Ps 20:2; 33:20; 70:5; 115:9-11; 121:1-2; 124:8). Eve was made of the "same

stuff" as Adam so that he at once recognized her as just
like himself. She was a helper "fit for him" (Gen 2:18 RSV).
The word *fit* can be translated "equal and corresponding
to."[2]

There is no hint of inequality between the sexes in Genesis 2. The man is told to leave father and mother and cleave
to his wife. The term used for *leave* means "to abandon" or
"forsake," and *cleave* means "to cling to."[3] When marriage
counselor Walter Trobisch taught these truths at Cam-
eroun Christian College in Africa,

> there was a real uproar in class. The wife should leave—
> that was understandable. In a patriarchal society, that
> goes without saying, just as it did in Israel. But that *man*
> should leave? Leave his father instead of continuing his
> life? No! Never! If a man leaves his father and mother—
> not leave them in the lurch, but leave them in order to
> establish his own home, his own family—instead of join-
> ing his family to the clan, he becomes economically inde-
> pendent.... Again the man cleaves to his wife, not the
> other way around only. The joining becomes mutual.
> And what is still just as important and revolutionary, a
> man cleaves to the *wife*, not to his clan.[4]

This standard for marriage, recorded in Genesis 2, is so
dramatically different from what many people have known
that it still causes tremors around the world. In the story of
the first couple we are given the perfect pattern of how God
intended man and woman to live together in harmony, not
hierarchy; in communion, not competition. It was this account that inspired John Milton to write:

> Two of far nobler shape erect and tall,
> God-like erect, with native honor clad
> In naked majesty seemed lords of all,
> And worthy seemed, for in their looks divine
> The image of their glorious Maker shone....

Simplicity and spotless innocence,
So passed they naked on, nor shunned the sight
Of God or angel, for they thought no ill;
So hand in hand they passed the loveliest pair
That ever since in love's embraces met.[5]

## Paradise Lost

On a sadder note, Milton also wrote: "Of Man's first disobe-
dience, and the fruit/ Of that forbidden tree, whose mortal
taste/ Brought death into the world, and all our woe."[6]
Paradise was lost the day the serpent tempted Eve to doubt
God's words and to disobey them, and Eve in turn tempted
Adam to do likewise (Gen 3:1-13). By doubting God's
words, they were doubting the integrity of their Maker.
When God confronted them with what they had done, they
both acted with characteristic fallenness and laid the blame
for their actions on someone else—Adam on Eve, and Eve
on the serpent. This game of locating evil outside ourselves
has been going on ever since.

We get a glimpse of the intimacy they had once known
with their Creator when we read, "The man and his wife
heard the sound of the LORD God as he was walking in the
garden in the cool of the day, and they hid from the LORD
God among the trees of the garden" (Gen 3:8). The two
who had known the joy of walking with God at the end of
the day—as friends often do—now tried to hide from the
reality of a broken relationship with that Friend.

Relationships were not only broken with God, but with
nature and between man and woman. Adam was told that
because of sin he and all other humans after him would
experience toil, thorns, thistles, sweat and death. Specifically given to Eve was the prediction of her pain in childbirth and the sad fact that the husband she would continue
to desire would rule over her. The oneness they had known
was destroyed by sin. From now on there would be a power

struggle between them (Gen 3:16).

As women found themselves the victims of this struggle, many of them acquired the "injured merit" syndrome of Milton's fallen angel.[7] Like the serpent, the woman began groaning, "I've been wounded." She ignored God's blessing of childbearing as a means of self-affirmation, for she was afflicted with the evil one's sin of pride. Therefore, instead of praising God—the purpose for which she was created—she complained.

All the complexities of evil started with the loss of paradise. Patricia Gundry in *Heirs Together* describes the cycle:

> The woman will more and more tend to rely upon her husband, be dependent upon him because of her many pregnancies and small children to care for, and as a result of her dependency, he will take advantage of her need and dominate her. I think it predicts the beginning of the true essence of worldliness: Those who are vulnerable look to the powerful for help, and the powerful exploit their power and rule over and mistreat the vulnerable. The process becomes complex and intertwines, extending itself geometrically until it has permeated all relationships.[8]

Since the day paradise was lost to Adam and Eve, many have tried to break this vicious cycle. Some have walked out on bad marriages. Even in the days when only one profession—prostitution—was open to women as an alternative to marriage, some women were desperate enough to choose it.

By the time Nora walked out on Torwald in Henrik Ibsen's *A Doll's House,* a number of professions were open to women, and yet she caused vibrations all over Europe with her dramatic exit; it was too shocking and unexpected in the age of Victorian complacency. What were her reasons?

> You have always been so kind to me. But our home has been nothing but a playroom. I have been your doll-wife,

just as at home I was papa's doll-child; and here the children have been my dolls. I thought it great fun when you played with me, just as they thought it great fun when I played with them. That is what our marriage has been, Torwald. . . . I believe that before all else I am a reasonable human being, just as you are—or—at all events—that I must try and become one.[9]

We have lived to see the new wave of women's liberation in our day and shared the heartaches as some of our friends and neighbors have followed in Nora's footsteps. They have seen this as the only solution to the put-down of women that started with the Fall. Meanwhile, the effect of their actions on their children is echoed in the counseling offices throughout the land. "Paradise lost" has only been intensified with more broken homes and more broken relationships each year. The cruel nightmare will be repeated in the next generation, and the next, and the next.

No wonder some among us react and call the nation back to the traditional marriage patterns of the past. But we fail to realize that these patterns were not necessarily any more Christian than the slavery our ancestors practiced so piously. We forget that when God broke into "paradise lost" and gave the Old Testament Laws, it was to temper social institutions like patriarchy, polygamy, divorce, slavery and monarchy. It did not mean that the Almighty ordained patriarchalism any more than he instituted slavery or divorce. We can thank God for mercifully stepping into our human condition to protect women after the Fall. There were laws to protect women from the whims of their husbands. Usually women under Judaism fared better than their pagan neighbors. But it was still the old order with all the bondages of the Law.

The Law was summed up in the two great commandments of love (Mt 22:37-40). Then Christ came as the fulfillment of that Law and brought "paradise regained." But since the time of Christ, many who have called themselves believers have rejected the new order Christ came to found. Some have been very sincere as they have struggled under the common limitations of seeing only "through a glass, darkly" (1 Cor 13:12 KJV). But often theologians have accepted the traditional structures of the Old Testament and missed the essence of both the Law and the gospel as they relate to women. That is why many still live in "paradise lost."

A friend of mine told me, "Without the chain of command in the home, we would have chaos." She was echoing the assumption that women will cause all manner of chaos unless ruled by men. Many modern theologians and other leaders maintain this view. One such Christian leader says that he has the power, according to Old Testament Law (Num 30), to nullify the vows his wife makes to the Lord.

> If your wife comes home and says she promised to teach Sunday School or sing in the choir or cook for the church supper, and you think this is a rash promise you are to tell her so—in love. It might go something like this: "Honey, I think you promised more than you can handle. We need you here at home." If she tells you she made the promise to the Lord, you are to say, "Yes, I know, but the Lord won't hold you to it, because I am your head and refuse to give you permission."[10]

Such teaching has produced a deep sense of unworthiness before God among women in evangelical circles. Looking on themselves as second-class Christians, they believe they are not entitled to the close personal relationship with Christ that their husbands may have. And since they always feel burdened with household chores, they give up, accepting the lie that they are not capable of being used by God in the proclamation of the good news.

Has the church put a tool in the husband's hand that is destructive? Christian sociologist John Scanzoni has said,

Power must always be tempered by justice or else it corrupts. . . . Who is to hold the husband accountable if not his wife? Who else can resist him when he is wrong? It is folly to assert "he is responsible to God." Kings, clergy and presidents with unchecked power become greedy and selfish and exploit others. The same is true of husbands with unchecked power.[11]

When the husband rules over the wife in spiritual and temporal matters he can become the mediator between his wife and her God. In the diagrams in some Christian books on marriage, there is no direct line between the wife and God. She only relates to God through her husband. As the son of close friends of ours put it, "My father serves God, and my mother serves my father." Such a patriarchal pattern becomes dangerous when submission to this system replaces submission to the lordship of Christ.

While some tend to make an idol out of a system, others may make idols out of their husbands. One of the most outspoken proponents of the traditional view of marriage speaks about husbands in the religious language that we commonly use only for God: "It is only when a woman surrenders her life to her husband, reveres and worships him, and is willing to serve him, that she becomes really beautiful to him."[12]

Another well-known writer goes a step further in equating her human husband with God incarnate:

One day this familiar verse acquired a heightened meaning for me, "Wives be subject to your husbands, as to the Lord" (Eph. 5:55). . . . I was to treat my own human husband as though *he* were the Lord, resident in our own humble home. . . . Would I ask Jesus a basically maternal question such as "How are things at the office?" Would I suggest to Jesus that He finish some tasks around the house? Would I remind the Lord that He was not driving prudently? Would I ever be in judgment over my Lord,

over His taste, His opinions, or His actions? I was stunned
—stunned into a new kind of submission.[13]
We must be very careful when we begin to tamper with a
woman's primary commitment to worship and serve the
Lord her God. She may lose her identity as a disciple.
Instead of Jesus Christ being her first love, she may end up
worshiping other gods: her husband, her children, and the
security of her home.

At a recent sharing meeting a young wife confessed, "I
realize that I have been making my husband my lord and
savior."

"And I don't make a very good lord and savior," her husband added. After that, with loyalties rearranged, they
were walking hand in hand with praise on their lips.

### Paradise Regained

Over three hundred years ago, Milton's imagination was
captured by the great theme of redemption as he wrote
his song of praise to the Son of the Most High in *Paradise
Regained:*

> A fairer Paradise is founded now
> For Adam and his chosen sons, whom thou
> A Savior art come down to reinstall; . . .
>
> Hail Son of the Most High, heir of both Worlds
> Queller of Satan, on thy glorious work
> Now enter, and begin to save mankind.[14]

When Jesus Christ came to earth to save mankind, we were
reinstated in paradise. "The old has gone, the new has
come," shouted Paul joyfully. For women, especially, everything changed when Jesus came. During the years that the
Savior walked on earth, the women who touched him and
conversed with him must have wondered if they were back

in paradise. Of course they were, for this was "paradise regained."

Only twice in history have we seen perfection in relationships between man and woman—in paradise and in the way Jesus interacted with women. But while we do not see complete perfection in human relationships today, we do see those who experience "paradise regained" because of their spontaneous openness to God's grace. How I thank God for the women I know who recognize that "it is for freedom that Christ has set us free," who "stand firm" and do not allow themselves to be "burdened again by a yoke of slavery" (Gal 5:1).

One of my best friends, Myrl Glockner, has been a great witness to the freedom she has found in Christ. Her freedom started when she began asking questions as a seventeen-year-old on a farm in Wisconsin where she grew up. "I was scared when I looked at people around me—the marriages of Christians didn't have what I wanted. And yet, marriage was the ultimate where I grew up," Myrl told me. She was through with school, but too young to work, so she stayed home with lots of time to think.

"What is there to life?" she asked herself. "When I get to be forty, will I look back and say, 'I wish I had done things differently'? I just didn't want to botch it up." As Myrl went through her spiritual search, she felt Christianity, as she saw it, lacked reality. She questioned Jesus, "If you are who you say you are, show me." The Lord answered her through a series of teachings on Romans in a local church. To her this was a witness that Jesus was real. So she turned her whole life over to Jesus Christ.

"I prayed that I would be kept from marriage till I knew the Lord was my satisfaction," she said. She claimed the promise that the Lord would satisfy her longing soul (Ps 107:1-9). God has fulfilled that promise to Myrl, who is today a model Christian woman. Jesus Christ has become her first love. She has loved and served her Lord, proclaiming the good news to hundreds through the Billy Graham Crusades and to thousands through Bible Study Fellowship. God has enlarged her heart to love her divine Lover, to love her husband, and to love the many to whom she ministers. Myrl is proof that a wife need not soft-pedal her relationship to Jesus Christ in order to make her husband feel secure in her love. And because of their dedication to God, Bob and Myrl reflect in their marriage the principles spelled out so graphically in Ephesians 5.

In this chapter, Paul first calls on all of us "to live a life of love, just as Christ loved us and gave himself up for us" (v. 2). Next comes the warning against sexual immorality, obscenity, impurity and drunkenness (3-18). Instead of getting drunk, believers should be "filled with the Spirit," which will result in praise: "Sing and make music in your heart to the Lord. . . . Speak to one another with psalms, hymns and spiritual songs. . . . Always giving thanks to God the Father for everything" (vv. 18, 19b, 19a, 20).

Within this context of praise and thanksgiving, we are called to "submit to one another out of reverence for Christ" (v. 21). Without repeating the word *submit* in the Greek text, Paul says in verse 22, "Wives, to your husbands as to the Lord." Paul knows that he is writing to women who are still living under a patriarchal system. As in the case of slavery (Eph 6:5-9), he is not ready to overthrow the sociological structure, but he is infusing it with a new type of love, *agapē*, which will take the sting out of patriarchalism and eventually replace it with Christ's model of servanthood

In the following verses (5:23-30), Paul calls on husbands to be servants of their wives as Christ was a servant to the church in the act of washing the disciples' feet. Paul wants the love of husbands for their wives to be as untarnished as Christ's love for the church. Paul states that the husband is the "head" of the wife. The word translated "head" is *kephalē* in the Greek text. This word can also mean "source," and the Mickelsens make a strong case for translating it that way.[15] Thus, Paul can be understood to be saying that husbands are the *source* of their wives, just as Christ is the *source* of the church. This would be an allusion to Genesis 2 and the formation of woman from Adam's side. Watchman Nee has suggested that the church was taken out of Christ's wounded side when he was buried and "slept" for three days before the resurrection.[16]

Again, alluding to Genesis 2, Paul calls on the husband to leave father and mother and cleave to his wife, "and the two will become one flesh. This is a profound mystery—but I am talking about Christ and the church" (vv. 31-32). What is implied in this "profound mystery"? How far can we carry the analogy between Christ's relationship to the church and the marriage relationship? Paul Jewett answers:

> The best statement of analogy . . . is not in terms of Christ's lordship over the church as the Savior of the body, for obviously husbands are not lords and saviors of their wives. . . . Rather the univocal element in the analogy, which helps us to grasp the mystery on which it is based, is the *henosis*, that is, the *oneness* which marks both the union between Christ and the church and between man and wife who become one flesh.[17]

The oneness is there because of *agapē*, the Calvary love Paul called believers to practice in verse 2: "Live a life of love, just as Christ loved us and gave himself for us." We can only love unconditionally if we give ourselves in the same way. *Agapē* involves commitment to love my spouse whether he deserves it or not.

Bob and I were startled when we arrived in the Philippines over twenty years ago and saw this type of love in action among Filipino Christians. They ignored my speeches on headship and hierarchy at women's meetings and just lived out a life of laying down their lives for one another. One woman, with a gambling husband, tried to voice her objections to my foreign theories. At first I dubbed her a rebel—until I was awed by her Christlike attitude of forgiving her husband and being totally committed to him.

The Filipinos also taught us something about practical decision making. I discovered that two people could receive the same message from God if they were listening to the same Voice. Thus Bob and I began to see the value of having two lines to God. When we received different messages, we knew we were confused and needed to pray longer before making a decision. And of course, when we got the same message, God's Word to us was confirmed as we both had heard the same Voice.

What a shock to come back to the States and have two pastors' wives tell me, "There's really no need to talk things over. You see, my husband makes all the decisions." I knew what they meant because I had once taught the same idea. I am glad that Bob and I have not only learned how to discuss and pray about decisions, but also how to open up about our hurts and misunderstandings. Through these experiences we have learned the mystery of asking for and offering forgiveness—as *agapē* operates between us. This love comes to us from God through an act of the will, not a feeling. It demands commitment.

Communication, confession and commitment are a few of the signposts on the road of a good marriage. But they need to be bathed in the sunlight of the unconditional love for each other which we receive as a gift from God every day. We have tried to tell our friends who talk of divorce that *agapē* is not the kind of love one can lose. In fact, it's always there for us to draw on, but sometimes we humans walk away from it—as we walk away from the light—into the darkness.

God has called all of us to penetrate the darkness with

the light of the good news. In the Philippines we were captivated by the couples who were "radical" about sharing the Light with others. Invariably they enjoyed the most fulfilling marriages. From them we learned the great principle of receiving back more than we ever give to others. Unlike the Christian marriage manuals that suggest we should concentrate on our own success and satisfaction in marriage, we found the more we reached out to others, the more our union was strengthened.

Today we thank God for the blueprints for marriage laid down in paradise. "What God has joined together" can last as long as the holy One gives us the *agapē* with which to love each other. Every step of the way we receive God's grace for our marriage and our ministry together. We are immensely grateful that this grace is operative so that Bob and I are good friends as well as lovers. It is as friends and lovers that we are learning to turn to the One who is our first love and to express our worship, adoration and praise. Our greatest moments together culminate in worship to the great God who created us, redeemed us and ushered us into "paradise regained."

# CHAPTER
# TWELVE

# Making Christ
# Head of the Home

**W**HEN I RETURNED FROM missionary work in the Philippines, I found that a focus of many sermons was the need to return to heterosexual relationships within the family. A common American assumption was that a strong father would counteract homosexual tendencies in his children. Thus, the father had taken a place of prominence within the family unit.

Naturally, I agreed with the emphasis on the sanctity of the marriage union, but I was mystified by statements such as, "I've been so blessed since I recognized my husband as the head of the house." I often expected to hear an account of the blessings of Christ's lordship in the speaker's life and home, but I was disappointed. Finally I started asking, "What's happened to Jesus around here?" It looked as if men had displaced Jesus Christ in the lives of women.

As I tried to decipher this conundrum, a typical Filipino village flashed across the screen of my memory. The houses were small and built of wood or bamboo, well-swept and surrounded by bougainvillea of every hue. I would walk down the clean, unpaved streets and glance through the open doors and windows where hand-crocheted curtains blew in the breeze. Home after home that wanted to declare to the world that they were Christians had this motto on the wall: Christ is the head of this house, the unseen Guest at every meal, the silent Listener to every conversation.

Remembering that motto, I called a local Christian bookstore and asked if such plaques were still being sold in the United States. "Oh, we used to have them years ago, but haven't had any in stock for a long, long time," I was told. I wondered how long it had been since some of my evangelical sisters in America had declared Christ as the head of their homes.

This was my first culture shock as I returned to the United States. My second soon followed as I went back to graduate school at the University of Minnesota. There I discovered that while I was worried about husbands replacing Jesus, my sisters in the women's study classes were preoccupied with the power struggle between men and women. And the home was attacked as one of the main bastions of male dominance.

As I listened to both sides of this issue, I longed to share the Christian message that Jesus gave man and woman a new identity when he died on the cross. This is good news for the home. Leveled at the cross, husband and wife return to that place daily to acknowledge their dependence on God's grace and to declare their love for Jesus Christ as the Lord of their lives and their homes.

This is the essence of Christianity, and here lies the secret of the happy home. Christ is the head and the center. Our hope and faith must be in the person of Christ rather than in a spiritualized human structure. While the patriarchal system may be workable for some families because of their cultural heritage, it is not this structure which makes a family Christian. A home is Christian only if Christ lives there and the family embraces his values to love each other and the oppressed poor of our world.

In the pages ahead we will consider some of the hindrances to letting Christ christianize our homes. We will also ask how we can learn to love the needy beyond our homes. The answer to this question is applicable not just to families but to the homes made up of single adults, like the home of Mary, Martha and Lazarus which Jesus loved to visit. (We probably have more information on this home and what went on there, than on any other home Jesus visited; see Lk 10:38-42; Jn 11:1-45 and 12:1-8.) However, since the majority of homes consist of adults and children, most of the problems discussed will center on those relationships.

## Who Is Boss?

If we think of Christ knocking on the door of every Christian home, what are the factors that complicate the simple process of opening the door and letting Christ enter to become the boss of our homes? Since we live in a real world, it is difficult to tune out all the other voices and listen only to the One knocking. Few homes have been untouched by the current hubbub caused by the power struggle between men and women.

Living in the age of the Equal Rights Amendment, we have seen the battle intensify. The home is often the arena. Each side has its cheerleading squad. The conservative church waves her arms with the traditionalists and shouts, "Men, be men. Don't give an inch. God is on your side . . . your side . . . your side."

Women's liberation also has its cheerleaders. They shout with even more vehemence, "Women, it's your turn to run the show. Don't lose the ground we've gained. Stand firm . . . stand firm . . . stand firm."

Children who grow up in Christian homes are caught in the crossfire of these two movements. No wonder they're confused! The issue becomes even more delicate as the mother and the father each undergo identity crises during the struggle. Often the man has been told that his identity depends on his being head of the home, while the woman hears that her identity requires breaking away from the patriarchal system of the past.

Many husbands and wives today are perched on a teeter-totter, going up and down with the latest slogans. I had been watching this motion for over a year after my return to the United States when I discovered a third force adding zest to the seesawing. I saw a little imp skipping back and forth, tipping the balance at unpredictable moments. As I watched the imp, it began to dawn on me that many American homes are not really run either by the husband or the wife. Instead, a hidden imp dictates the actions. Jesus called the imp *mammon* and put him in opposition to God: "Ye cannot serve God and mammon" (Mt 6:24 KJV).

Meanwhile, the world sings ditties about the imp. "Money makes the world go 'round," runs a song ("Money, Money") by John Kander and Fred Ebb. Dollars and marks, yens and pounds, all make "that clinking, clanking sound,"[1] an audible symbol of the power of money to get our attention and control our lives.

Part of making the world go 'round is the way money is used to grease the wheels of family life. For instance, a husband may believe his manhood depends on being the boss at home. In his struggle to be recognized, he is easily tricked into seeking the help of the imp. After all, money means power in this world. Why not use this power to pad the tottering patriarchal system? I have seen many a sincere man trying to improve his self-image before his family, as well as his peers, through money. Using this power easily becomes a substitute for finding his true self in relationship to Jesus Christ.

And women fall right into the same trap as more and more families capitulate to the modern fad of two salaries. The imp has told them they cannot pay their bills with one. Some women are asked by their husbands to work. Others go to work in spite of their husband's protests. Many women feel worthless until they can compete in the job market. The radical feminists reinforce this by reminding women that jobs are useless unless a dollar sign is attached.

In the *Equal Rights Monitor,* a not-so-funny comic strip shows one woman telling another, "If I spend my days cleaning bathtubs and toilets, my status as a female is equal to a groveling worm.... But if I go to work for the sewer company, I'll make headlines as a feminist star.... What makes the same measly job an insult if you do it at home, but an honor if you make it a career!!?"

The answer comes back in one word, "Money."[2]

Housework and volunteer work have both been so played down that even the wealthiest matron has to chase the almighty dollar to keep her self-respect. Imagine the impression left on a child who lives in a home where two parents are trying to prove their worth to themselves and to each other by the size of the paychecks that they bring home.

In contrast, Jesus said, "If a man will let himself be lost for my sake, he will find his true self. What will a man gain by winning the whole world at the cost of his true self?" (Mt 16:25-26 NEB). By serving the imp, some parents have not only lost their true selves, but also their children. Through the protests of the sixties, children screamed at their parents that they were tired of their materialistic values. Today, some of those very protesters have fallen into the same trap as they have become parents. It is easy for parents to try to build security structures for their children made of wood, hay and stubble instead of gold, silver and precious stones (1 Cor 3:12).

"I built the swimming pool to keep my kids home," a wealthy doctor confided. One of the kids had already told me that it would take more than a swimming pool to put their family together again. Others try building basements big enough to house their son's band, or summer cottages where the kids can bring their friends during vacations. For others, getting their kids away from their friends is the goal, and so they plan elaborate family vacations to Mexico, Europe or the Caribbean. All the while the true values of love, joy and peace—the gold, silver, and precious stones of life—are forgotten.

As a new parent I had my first warning of this danger when I relaxed in a Chicago hospital after the birth of my first baby. The attractive woman in the next bed was talking: "My mother always worked in all the years I can remember. She had no time for me."

I was intensely interested. Eager to establish the perfect home for my newborn, this was just the topic I wanted to discuss.

She continued, "Mother worked long and odd hours at a supermarket cash register. She bought me lots of clothes and toys, and finally a horse. I had everything except what I wanted most. I always wished she'd have the time to notice me."

The "poor little rich girl" has always been the child who has everything and nothing, whether her mother works at a cash register or belongs to the jet set. What she lacks is her parent's love expressed through high-quality time with her. Often her mother does not work, but still has no time for her. And of course, there are mothers who work who give adequate time to their children evenings and weekends. This is not an attack on working mothers, but a search into the motivation for working. Is the imp tipping the balance?

Christian mothers may be participating unwittingly in building a home run by the imp rather than by the principles of Jesus Christ. When a family's values are tied to the dollar sign, a loyalty to the patriarchal or egalitarian system will not change the quality of their lives. Only Christ is the unifying Person who can change persons so they can find their true selves. In the process they will become partakers of his divine nature, which is love. This is the greatest value change in the world. And once the door to change has been opened, the heart of each member of the family can be enlarged to love and care for the needy beyond their door.

## When Jesus Christ Is Head of the Home

All sorts of changes take place when Jesus is the boss, but the greatest is the change of values. Just as a dog loses interest in the dry bone he has been gnawing on all day when offered a steak, so the Christian discovers the worthlessness of material possessions when offered the adventure of sharing with the world's oppressed people. Even living frugally and saving for the family is not enough without making the most of our resources for the good of the larger family of God. No longer is the nuclear family tied into the myopic vision of a patriarch and his clan, but we may enlarge our vision because Jesus is now the Head. Now we may save for our larger family of God's people around the world, most of whom are poor!

Such an outlook stands in direct opposition, not only to the materialists who accumulate wealth, but also to those who preach austerity for its own sake. We all know of selfish people who have chosen a simple lifestyle to accomplish some personal goal. The poor have not benefited from their lower standard of living. When Jesus calls us to a new lifestyle the poor will benefit. We will have definite goals for trimming our budgets, our wardrobes, our freezers and our figures. Like many who tightened their belts in time of war, we have the same goal: to defeat our enemy and save our people.

Today our warfare is waged against the one who is behind all oppression of the poor in this world. Without the rich to oppress them, there would be no poor. As the rich submit to the dominion of the god of this world, the rich get richer and the poor get poorer. Jesus picks up on the same note as did the prophets in the Old Testament when he says: "Blessed are you who are poor. . . . But woe to you who are rich. . . . Blessed are you who hunger now. . . . Woe to you who are well fed now. . . . Blessed are you who weep now. . . . Woe to you who laugh now. . . . Woe to you when all men speak well of you, for that is how their fathers treated the false prophets" (Lk 6:20, 24, 21a, 25, 21b, 26).

Some of the same people who listened to these words of Jesus had already heard John the Baptist's challenge to repentance. "What should we do then?" they asked John.

"The man with two tunics should share with him who has none, and the one who has food should do the same," comes the blunt answer (Lk 3:11). But what shall *we* do in a clothes-crazy country like America? Perhaps we can start by not worrying about wearing the same outfit each time we go to church or to a party. Where does the value come from that says we should wear something new for every special occasion? Maybe we could ask ourselves about our values when we are ready to write a check or pull out a credit card in a store: do I need this, or should this amount go to someone who is hungry?

The next question is how to teach such concepts to children. It can be done only by example. My husband will never forget the year in his childhood when his father did not buy a new suit, even though his best Sunday outfit was getting threadbare. The money went to missions instead. Ron Sider calls Christians to such action in his book *Rich Christians in an Age of Hunger:* "If a mere fraction of North American and European Christians would begin to apply biblical principles on economic sharing among the world-wide people of God, the world would be utterly astonished."[3] On the other hand, when we accumulate more wealth than we need, we are like the people in the Old Testament who hoarded the manna. Suddenly the blessing of God's provision became a curse! The manna they had hoarded began to stink (Ex 16:1-20). Do we want homes that stink, or homes filled with the fragrance of Jesus Christ who is the boss of our lives and our bank accounts?

In order for Christ to become the Head of our homes, we need to consider the priorities of our lives. We need to study God's Word together, and as we do, passages about reaching out to others in love will strike us (for example, Mt 25:31-46; Lk 10:25-37; Acts 2:42-47; 4:32-37; 11:27-30; and the book of James).[4] Then we can try to put some of the things we've learned about priorities into action. Maybe our lifestyles will change by giving up ice cream or coffee, or taking in strangers, like refugees or foreign students. The child or adult who never has had to relate to people who are "not our kind" is truly poverty stricken. God has great wealth in store for us as we bring the poor and the stranger into the inner circle of our homes.

But opening our homes to people means more than sharing the physical comforts with those in need. After we have developed a relationship of trust with an individual, the greatest treasure we have to share with that person is our identification with Jesus Christ. That's why Paul wrote: "Christ's love compels us, because we are convinced that one died for all. . . . And he died for all, that those who live should no longer live for themselves. . . . If anyone is in

Christ, he is a new creation; the old has gone, the new has come! All this is from God, who reconciled us to himself through Christ and gave us the ministry of reconciliation" (2 Cor 5:14-15, 17-18).

Once we have discovered the path of reconciliation with God, we are compelled by love to point the way for others. There may be many women around us who are aching and hurting because of the poverty and injustice we have been discussing here. Or they may be isolated from loved ones because of a lack of reconciliation, a lack of *agape*. This loneliness and conflict may lead to nervous breakdowns or divorce. We as God's reconciled children can bring the good news of his unconditional love for them.

Our loving Lord always looked on people as whole persons. He never divided the needs of the body from those of the soul, as we sometimes do. To the crowds who came to hear him he gave bread when they were hungry—bread for the body and the living Bread. He healed the paralytic and told him, "Your sins are forgiven." Can we do less for those whom we take into our hearts and homes?

Jesus calls us to love as he loved. Thus, an open home where Christ is the head can be a place of healing. Many women have found that people may be more open to God's love when it is shared in the nonthreatening atmosphere of a cozy living room. These same people would not perhaps go to church, and if a stranger tried to talk to them about God, they would view it as an invasion of privacy. But coffee and Bible study at a neighbor's home is different because people can sense the dynamics of love.

We read in Acts that the believers daily "continued to meet together in the temple courts. They broke bread in their homes and ate together with glad and sincere hearts, praising God and enjoying the favor of all the people. And the Lord added to their number daily those who were being saved" (2:46-47). Could it be that neighbors, relatives and friends popped in on the believers in their homes to see what was going on? Today we once more need to eat together as Christians and preach the gospel in our homes. Only when our houses become shining beacons for the Lord will it be clear to the world around us that the authority at home rests with the right Person.

# CHAPTER THIRTEEN

# Sharing Christ in Society

**H**AVING SPENT MY HIGH-school years in a British boarding school in China that was well staffed with servants to polish our shoes and floors, I was hardly qualified to take on a Saturday housecleaning job in college. But I needed the money to pay my tuition so I started working for a wealthy Chicago socialite who loved to listen to the Metropolitan Opera on Saturday afternoons.

Each time the music came over the airwaves, Mrs. Hutton would quiver with excitement and interrupt my cleaning to discuss the opera. Eager to please, I decided to read the paper beforehand to get the details of the story of the day. Mrs. Hutton was overjoyed that she had found someone who shared her enthusiasm for the music she loved so well.

One Saturday, however, there was no time for the opera, as she had to rush off to a social function. Walking out the door, she shouted her last instructions for the day, "You'll find the wax for the kitchen floor in a vinegar bottle in the basement." I searched and re-searched that basement for a bottle containing what I imagined wax would look like, but to no avail. There were too many vinegar bottles, each containing some unknown liquid. Finally, I settled on a pink substance which formed neat little sand piles on the floor and refused to shine. But then who was I to judge what strange shape wax might take?

I forgot about the pink "wax" until an accusing Mrs. Hutton met me at the back door the next Saturday with, "Do you know that I had to get down on my hands and knees— me with my terrible arthritis—to clean up the silver polish? You mean you don't know what wax looks like?" Since I wanted neither to reveal my ignorance nor to tell a lie, I mumbled something about how sorry I was for having caused her such pain. I was searching for some polite parting remark when Mrs. Hutton suddenly changed her mood.

"I'm going to let you stay," she said with determination. "Obviously you are useless at housework, but I enjoy having an intelligent person around on Saturdays to discuss the opera." I looked at her in astonishment, and then I understood. She was lonely and longed for someone to talk to. I had entered her little world and become part of it; she did not want to lose her new friend. I had been reaching out unknowingly to someone lonely and needy in the community.

We have the lonely rich, like Mrs. Hutton, and the lonely poor. The neglected can be young or old, single or married—for example, a couple struggling to keep their family together and feeling that nobody cares. There are the lonely sick, and the even more lonely aliens. The list is endless! How can a woman of God remain in the security of her home and ignore such needs? A person committed to Jesus Christ will be compelled to reach out beyond herself and her family. She will have opportunities through her career or volunteer work to minister to the lonely, hurt and needy, using all the gifts and talents God has given her. She will become a catalyst for change, a healing agent and a prophetic voice in our hurting world.

Several obstacles seem to keep women from reaching out beyond themselves. We will consider these and see how God desires to use women to lay down their lives for others.

### "A Woman's Place Is in the Home"

The slogan "A woman's place is in the home" has become a major obstacle to women's outreach. There is nothing specifically Christian about this slogan. The same opinion is expressed in various parts of the world. When my sister-in-law was a new missionary in China, a kindly Chinese woman came to stay with her and her new baby. In her limited Chinese, my sister-in-law asked her about the bound feet among women in China. "Oh, the men want it that way so we won't go too far away from the house. They don't want us involved in life beyond the home," was the matter-of-fact reply. Perhaps she was paraphrasing the Chinese proverb: "Feet are bound, not to make them beautiful as a curved bow, but to restrain women when they go out of doors."[1]

As a child in China, I remember my curiosity getting the better of me during a similar discussion with an old woman I loved dearly. I asked to see her feet and stood there awed as she unwound her bandages. Her stump of a foot had not grown since as a baby her feet had been tied with bandages and wire, so they would stay small and she would stay home. Questioning my assertion that the concept is a pagan one, a Bible professor once asked me as we sipped coffee together, "But don't you believe a woman's place is in the home?"

"Of course I do if there are loved ones around who need

her," I answered. "But she should not stay home just to stay home. Do you think women should be home to watch the woodwork or the TV?"

Why then did Paul tell the women of Crete to stay home and love their families (Tit 2:4-5)? The Cretans were called "liars, evil brutes, lazy gluttons" by one of their own prophets (1:12). So there were probably women among them who were neglecting their homes and families. We have already discussed how married women in Greek culture were secluded and had little opportunity to socialize outside the home or to communicate with their husbands. It is thus understandable that some women did not feel any strong sense of responsibility for their husbands or homes. At religious festivals these women had their big chance to leave the house and participate. When such women became Christians it was easy for them to look on church gatherings as opportunities to escape the boredom of home life. Paul recommends a new form of life for these women where love will replace their indifference for their homes and husbands.

If Paul were alive today, however, given his obsession with preaching the gospel, would he not urge women to take advantage of their new status in the modern world? Unlike those ancient women, women today can lecture in universities, ascend the podium at political rallies and wield the gavel at court. The great apostle would remind us that this is the greatest age to be a Christian woman because we can now enter society as professional workers and concerned citizens without worrying about going against the cultural norm of our age.

One minister who preaches to seven thousand each week in his California church believes strongly that today women belong at home. He tells women: "The Bible gives you identity from your children and your family. . . . It's always been that way . . . older women teaching the young women to love their husbands and their children and to be keepers at home."[2] This man cites one passage in Titus and cancels all the other commandments given to men and women.

By contrast, when Jesus gave his last orders to the men and women who were present at his ascension, the lost and hurting world, not the home, was the focus of his Great Commission. Jesus' last words were no surprise to the men and women present because they had seen Jesus' model of ministry as he traveled around the countryside with his disciples and the faithful women who had left their homes to join him in spreading the good news (Lk 8:1-3). And Jesus had told these men and women that they were not to put their faith or invest their identities in temporal things (and even husbands, children and careers are temporal), but in the eternal treasures of heaven.

Jesus had taught about the conflict of interest between relationships at home and what it meant to follow Jesus: "If anyone comes to me and does not hate her father and mother, her husband and children, her brothers and sisters —yes, even her own life—she cannot be my disciple.... Any of you who does not give up everything she has cannot be my disciple" (Lk 14:26, 33, my changes).

In China, woman evangelist Marie Monsen wondered if women would ever be released to follow Christ as their first love. She wrote about the 1920s:

> There were so few women in the churches. From time immemorial Chinese women had been home-keepers and they still were. "Home-keeper" was the word used for "woman" in the common speech. Prayer rose from the depths of our hearts in that hour for the women of China. One of us had received a word from the Lord: "The Lord giveth the word: the women that publish the tidings are a great host" (Psalm 68:11 R.V.)....And we saw it fulfilled. All the unrest caused by continual bandit attacks forced the "home-keepers" of China out of

their homes. They grew accustomed to flee at a moment's notice, accustomed to walking about in the open and being seen.... Christian women had marvellous opportunities of meeting heathen women fleeing from their ravaged homes and were able to be the Lord's witnesses to them in time of trouble. The first time I saw how the unrest was turning into a fulfillment of the word that had been given to us is an unforgettable moment.... What a sight it was! The congregation was five times as large as we had ever seen it, and three out of every five among them were women.... Political unrest had ploughed deep furrows across ancient traditions and prejudices.[3]

Sometimes I wonder if it is going to take the ravages of war to get the modern Christian American woman out of her home and her preoccupation with the trivia of housekeeping and hobbies into the hurting world that needs her love and her message. Her home has become like her saltshaker. How can her salt get out of the shaker and into the world?[4] When Jesus told men and women to "go into all the world and preach the gospel," the Savior of the world was thinking of both geographical locations around the earth and all walks of life—all vocations and professions. Such doors are open today for women all over the world in a way that the women of China in the 1920s could not have imagined.

But obviously, entering the job market does not necessarily lead to fruitful Christian witness. There are still obstacles that keep women from using their gifts most fruitfully for Christ.

### Barriers beyond the Home
The misconception that the reward is found not in the work she does, but in the money she gets, has kept many a woman from the vocation or the volunteer work for which

she has special aptitude. Unfortunately, our society has been so penetrated with materialistic values that women are often discouraged from pursuing careers that fascinate them because the preparation will be too costly or the financial reward too little. The same value system has persuaded another large group of women to quit volunteer work and look for "anything that pays" to fill the empty hours during the years that they are no longer needed full time at home.

As long as a woman views her work hours as only a time to make money, she contradicts the basic Christian assumption that all the hours of the day belong to God, and everything she does—using the talents endowed by her Creator —can be offered to God as a sacred service. Many modern Christians think as Christians only on Sundays. As long as God is taken care of in the sacred Sunday box, the rest of the week can be devoted to secular pursuits. Such an attitude dilutes the verbal and nonverbal witness of Christian women in society.

But where does such an attitude come from? Perhaps C. S. Lewis had a key when he wrote *The Screwtape Letters*. At one point Screwtape warns the apprentice devil how to handle a new believer:

As long as he does not convert it into action, it does not matter how much he thinks of this new repentance. . . . Let him do anything but act. No amount of piety in his imagination and affections will harm us if we can keep it out of his will. . . . Active habits are strengthened by repetition but passive ones are weakened. The more often he feels without acting, the less he will be able ever to act, and, in the long run, the less he will be able to feel.[5]

The serpent aims to make Christians insensitive to the nudging of God's Spirit and the calls for help from fellow humans. Love for God and love for neighbor always go hand in hand. Both are affected by the serpent's efforts to keep repentance out of the will so that Christians will be hearers on Sundays, and not doers seven days a week.

Paul spoke to this issue when he told the Romans: "Offer your bodies as living sacrifices, holy and pleasing to God— which is your spiritual worship. Do not conform any longer to the pattern of this world, but be transformed by the renewing of your mind. Then you will be able to test and approve what God's will is—his good, pleasing and perfect will" (12:1-2). Worship is described here in terms of surrender of the will—my will to God's will—every day of the week. We are created to worship and praise only one God, to love and adore only one God. When this relationship becomes a reality, all our work in the secular world is transformed into spiritual worship. And the call to a particular job for the Christian woman becomes synonymous with a call to divine service.

### Serving God through a Career

Again merging worship and work, Paul wrote to the Colossians: "Let the word of Christ dwell in you richly as you teach and admonish one another with all wisdom, and as you sing psalms, hymns and spiritual songs with gratitude in your hearts to God. And whatever you do, whether in word or deed, do it all in the name of the Lord Jesus, giving thanks to God the Father through him" (3:16-17). Paul goes on to address the Christians in the most difficult of all occupations: "Slaves. . . . Whatever you do, work at it with all your heart, as working for the Lord, not for men, since you know that you will receive an inheritance from the Lord as a reward. It is the Lord Christ you are serving" (3:22-24).

If even slaves could look on their work as an offering to God, surely most of us can do the same when we find ourselves in situations where we feel the sting of prejudice. Women, like slaves, are often reminded that they are in a position of weakness in the marketplace. Each woman needs to be aware of these attitudes, and take a stand against them, while keeping the beautiful spirit of servant-hood *to the Lord* expressed by Paul to the slaves. As Christians, we live with the promise that the same gospel that has dealt the death blow to chattel slavery will do likewise to the injustices women endure in the job market. Thanks be to God that "there is neither . . . slave nor free, male nor female, for you are all one in Christ Jesus" (Gal 3:28).

However, most Christian women have more problems with their own inner attitudes towards a career than they have with the prejudices from without. Some of these attitudes have been fostered by the church. Evangelical women have sometimes been discouraged from exploring career goals. College is often looked on as a time to find a man, rather than a time to prepare to love God and our neighbors through a career. And there is the unspoken threat that if a woman steps outside her sphere (homemaking, nursing, teaching, typing), she may lose her femininity. Women have been trained to hide their talents and consequently some of them have denied the Lord's call to action.

As I have talked to middle-aged women at retreats about the use of their talents, I have seen them weep and gnash their teeth as they admit their sense of failure and uselessness. Most of these women confess that they had never thought of God's unique plan for their lives beyond finding the right mate. It is true that God's plan for the majority of women includes motherhood, but since the average family in the United States has only two children, full-time motherhood (when the children are home all day) fills less than ten years of a woman's life.

Gail Sheehy tells us that thirty-five is the age when the average mother sends her last child off to school. She adds that the same year

> the average married American woman re-enters the working world. Census figures show she can then expect

to be part of the work force for the next twenty-four years or more. Few homemakers are prepared for that thunderbolt. There is no mention in high school of what comes after the proper selection of a husband, household appliances, and schools for the children: twenty-four years of using the skills she had the good sense or accidental fortune to acquire before she got married—or —twenty-four years of being a sales fixture or operator 47. No one tells girls that motherhood is only half a life-work.[6]

For the Christian, the money or prestige the job brings is not the issue. Finding God's unique design for all of her life is. But somehow, finding that unique purpose for which she is created is tied up with a woman's sense of identity. In *Passages* Sheehy laments the fact that many women postpone their expansion, or the discovery of their unique identity, as long as the children keep them busy. "Each passage [phase of life] raises the issue anew, and if it is not resolved, eventually the pilot light goes out and something begins to foul the air."[7]

We have all met middle-aged women in whom the light seems to have gone out. They have never really found their own identity, and they have postponed the expansion of that identity till it seems too late. The feminists are right in their war cry that women need to think of their expansion early in life. Non-Christian women who look on themselves as unique creations with special talents for special tasks often seem to be more "together," with a far stronger sense of identity than their evangelical sisters with low self-images. For the latter, coming to Christ has just meant taking the first step. The next step is responding to the Lord's call to use their gifts and talents to help others in and beyond the home.

As Christian women we will find our identity only in a relationship with Jesus Christ. This relationship will enable us to break out of our culturally bound identities, to minister as catalysts for change, prophetic voices or healing agents in the homes, churches and societies of our hurting world. If a disciple of Jesus lacks this sense of identity and has no special calling in life, it is very unlikely that anyone will ask her to "give the reason for the hope that you have" (1 Pet 3:15). Her verbal and nonverbal witness will be jeopardized.

In order to find out what their special assets are, many Christians are going through courses like the one outlined in *The Truth about You*. This course helps Christians determine what tasks they are good at and which ones they enjoy so they can use their assets to the fullest extent and to God's glory.[8]

## Serving God through Volunteer Work

Whether we serve God through a career or through volunteer work, we need to open our minds and hearts to discover God's special design for us. While talents can often surface through vocational testing, discovery of our spiritual gifts depends on openness to the Holy Spirit, operating through the church, as we follow biblical guidelines. The numerous gifts given to Christians are always given for the upbuilding of the church and the proclamation of the good news with its resulting benefits for the world. As we look at the lists of gifts given in Romans 12:4-8, 1 Corinthians 12:12-31, Ephesians 4:11-13 and 1 Peter 4:10-11, we see that gifts are never given for the benefit of the individual Christian. Some women have verbal gifts like teaching and preaching, while others function better in activities like administration, leadership, healing, serving, encouraging, contributing to the needy, and showing mercy and hospitality.

Christians tend to forget that, instead of listing the gifts, Jesus listed the situations in the world where the gifts of the church are most needed: among the hungry, the naked, the sick, the imprisoned, the lonely or strangers (Mt 25: 31-46). If evangelical women would follow Jesus' call into all these areas of need, they could help prevent poor teenagers from beginning a pattern of crime, comfort the lonely and troubled, and bring hope to prison cells and hospital rooms.

In the Philippines I saw on a large scale what God intended every Christian home to be—a home open to poor relatives, including cousins ten times removed, a home open to unknown travelers from one's home town region, and a home open to the refugees always on the move because of civil strife. These Christian homes were places where people were always ready to share floor space and the last pot of rice. Because of poverty the library in such a home might consist of two books: the Bible and the hymnbook. Yet what wealth these Christians had to share with their visitors when after the evening meal the two books would be brought to the table. God's Word would be read and discussed, followed by a hymn and prayer. The women usually took their turns in leading these family worship sessions that often resulted in the conversion of some of the visitors. The sharing of rice and floor space went hand in hand with sharing the good news. "I was a stranger and you invited me in," said Jesus.

What is the reward for women who give their lives in service for others? Not the dollar sign that some have placed on a woman's contribution to society. The Christian woman takes literally the words of her Savior: "What good is it for a woman to gain the whole world, and yet lose or forfeit her very self? . . . For whoever wants to save her life will lose it, but whoever loses her life for me will save it" (Lk 9:25, 24, my changes).

Christ's profit and loss values stand in sharp contrast to those of the secular world and those so often embraced by the evangelical church. To the faithful the Savior promises nothing but the joy of service. The service itself is the reward! It is a privilege to lay down our lives in a variety of ways for someone else within or beyond our families. After demonstrating the joy of doing a menial task, washing the feet of his disciples, Jesus promised the disciples the great reward: "Now that you know these things, you will be blessed if you do them" (Jn 13:17).

Jesus explains in the story of the last judgment that a first-love relationship with the King *will* result in love for our neighbors also. Because of love for the King, we will reach out beyond our families as catalysts for change and healing agents in the hurting society around us. "I tell you the truth, whatever you did for one of the least of these . . . , you did for me" (Mt 25:40).

# CHAPTER FOURTEEN

# Women in the Eleventh Hour

**M**Y FIVE-YEAR-OLD BROTH-
er was wiggling more than usual through the long sermon
in church in our home town of Kristiansand, Norway. He
whispered, "Let's go home, Mamma, I've heard all this
before. I know it all by heart." As a missionary child he
was probably right. He had heard it all before on the Sunday mornings and evenings he had been taken regularly
to church. But did that mean that the truths he had heard
had transformed his life by the time he was five?

The question I want to look at in this remaining chapter
is whether or not our acknowledged need for a first-love
relationship with Jesus Christ has radically changed us as
women. When Jesus traveled from one town and village to
another proclaiming the good news of the kingdom of God,
he told the men and women who followed him, "Consider

carefully how you listen. Whoever has will be given more; whoever does not have, even what she thinks she has will be taken from her" (Lk 8:18, my changes). Could Jesus have been saying that if a woman listens, applying what she hears and taking responsibility for the proclamation of the gospel, more truth will be revealed to her and more gifts and opportunities to exercise them will be given to her? And could Jesus also be warning women that not to apply or obey what we hear will mean that the revelation, gifts and responsibilities that we think we have, will be taken from us?

We have seen in this book how some women have begun to function as catalysts for change, as prophetic voices, and as healing agents because of their love for Jesus Christ. They have discovered that as they took the first tiny steps of faith, their gifts have been identified and new doors have been opened for a wider ministry. Such women are needed now in the eleventh hour when our world cries for every believer to participate in the great harvest.

Jesus dramatized this explosive truth in the parable of the vineyard (Mt 20:1-16). The landowner went out five different times to hire workers for his vineyard. He asked the last group, those in the eleventh hour, "Why have you been standing here all day long doing nothing?"

"Because no one has hired us," they answered. They were invited to join in the harvest, and they were given the same wages as those who had worked all day long. We are not told why these workers were not hired earlier, but the landowner was gracious and paid them for a full day's work.

Fredrik Franson, founder of The Evangelical Alliance Mission, has suggested that perhaps these workers were women.[1] Scripture does not tell us. But we might surmise that these latecomers were wives and single women and daughters and mothers who previously were not asked to join the harvest. Now the time is late, and the Lord is calling us to work because the church, at least in some cases, has neglected to call us. Jesus' concern is reaping the harvest. And it is time for us to join the work.

What are our wages? The wage is not in coins to be counted but in abundant and indivisible joy. To be called to work in the vineyard is the chief way God can bless his followers, for "there is joy in serving Jesus." The joy of serving begets more serving. Therefore, we can expect that the wages paid the eleventh-hour workers will result in an explosion of possibilities for service never dreamed of by the women of the past. Spiritual reproduction is another way of describing this service. Robert Coleman writes:

> By the blood of the Lamb the church is victorious. Believing the Gospel commits one to proclaim it. Thus, built into the saving message is the principle of reproduction. ... What a masterful plan of conquest! When the Son of God is lifted up by His followers, hearers of the Word are called to believe on Him.... Through this simple process of multiplication, nothing in this world can keep the church from storming the gates of hell.[2]

As women we show our love for Jesus Christ by being on the offensive in this battle. We can announce, like Peter and Martha (Mt 16:16; Jn 11:27), that Jesus is the Christ, the Son of God, and claim the promise that the gates of hell will not overcome this rock of truth.

Jesus said, "Go into all the world and preach the good news to all creation" (Mk 16:15). The verb *preach* comes from the Latin "to proclaim."[3] Jesus declared that all Christians are to be witnesses, proclaiming his good news to all people (Acts 1:8), including women.

### How Will We Serve?
Whether we call it preaching or sharing, we will be declaring the good news within the context of our spiritual gifts. 1 Corinthians 12 tells us that each of us has a gift:

In each of us the Spirit is manifested in one particular
way, for some useful purpose.... For Christ is like a
single body with its many limbs and organs, which, many
as they are, together make up one body.... A body is not
one single organ, but many.... If the whole were one
single organ, there would not be a body at all; in fact,
however, there are many different organs, but one body.
... Now you are Christ's body, and each of you a limb
or organ of it. Within our community God has appointed, in the first place apostles, in the second place prophets, thirdly teachers; then miracle-workers, then those
who have gifts of healing, or ability to help others or
power to guide them, or the gift of ecstatic utterance of
various kinds (vv. 7, 12, 15, 19-20, 27-28 NEB).

With these gifts comes the responsibility to use them:

The identifying of gifts brings to the fore ... the issue of
commitment. Somehow, if I name my gift and it is confirmed, I cannot "hang loose" in the same way. I would
much rather be committed to God in the abstract than to
be committed to him at the point of my gifts.... Com-
mitments at the point of my gifts means that I must give
up being a straddler.... Life will not be the smorgasbord
I have made it, sampling and tasting here and there. My
commitment will give me an identity.[4]

Our identity as women of God is tied to our gifts and our
consequent commitment of them to Jesus Christ for his
church. Once we have seen the world from our Lord's perspective, especially in the eleventh hour of our history, how
can we ever return to a vision that is limited to the traditional roles of women? Stephen Clark, a leader in the
Catholic charismatic movement, has said, "One term which
Paul uses to describe the gifts is 'service' (1 Cor. 12:5). The
gifts are not gifts to the individual Christian. They are gifts
*through* the individual Christian to the community. For the
individual Christian they are a service, a service he can per-

form for the community."[5]

## Where Will We Serve?

Where should women serve the Lord? The answers are as many as the places on earth. While a woman's ministry need not be limited to her home, it must always begin there. Then it will reach out in ever-widening circles, according to the Acts 1:8 principle: "But you will receive power when the Holy Spirit comes on you; and you will be my witnesses in Jerusalem, and in all Judea, and Samaria, and to the ends of the earth."

I was reminded of our responsibility to be witnesses in our homes as I talked to a woman who had waited through the raising of six children for her husband to initiate family devotions. Now her children are gone, and I suggested that she should wait no longer to function as a priest in her own home. Since her husband is a godly man, I assured her he would probably be relieved and happy to join her in prayer and Bible reading at their breakfast table. "Start tomorrow," I urged her. She promised she would.

Family worship is a beautiful opportunity for the woman of God to share her love for Jesus Christ with her family. Even when the husband is not a believer, he may be awed by her devotion to her Lord as she combines this with a life of *agape* love and service to her family. Fredrik Franson suggests the necessity of both the verbal and nonverbal witness in the home:

> Some have objected that Peter has said that the husbands would be won without words through the wives' quiet conversation (1 Peter 3:1). It is clear that a wife cannot incessantly talk (nag) her husband into conversation. Her word in that way loses its power and in such situations her conduct speaks louder than her words. . . . The Word should of course be the first means that the wives should use in order to win them, but if that does not succeed,

they should believe that through their quiet conduct
they can bring blessing to their husbands.[6]
Any woman who puts Christ first will become a better wife,
daughter, mother and homemaker. She will share the good
news with her own family and anyone else to whom the
home is open. But a woman's witness does not stop there.

Many women, like my mother in China, have followed
the pattern of Paul who taught "publicly and from house to
house" (Acts 20:20). Franson gives a rationale for this
method of evangelism:

> If the one who engages in house visitation finds quite
> soon that she cannot visit more than a half dozen or a
> dozen families without becoming very tired and having
> to again and again answer the same type of objection,
> how much easier then to be able at one time to speak to all
> of these?[7]

Other women will be witnesses to Christ in their vocations
or as they perform voluntary service. Catherine Booth
combined a loving concern for others with a verbal witness
to the gospel. Throughout her life, as cofounder of the
Salvation Army, Catherine Booth was involved in everything from preaching to crowds and visiting drunkards, to
factory legislation and championing the needs of England's
poor. She warned women of "tattle and tea-parties" and
"light reading" and challenged them to serious discipleship
and loyalty to Jesus Christ.[8]

Writing for the *Methodist New Connection Magazine* before
her marriage, she said:

> There seems . . . a growing disinclination among female
> members to engage in prayer, speak in love feasts and
> band meetings, or in any manner bear testimony for
> their Lord. . . . And this false, God-dishonoring timidity
> is but too fatally pandered to by the Church, as if God
> had given any talent to be hidden in a napkin. . . . Why
> should the swaddling-bands of blind custom, which in

Wesley's days were so triumphantly broken, and with such glorious results thrown to the moles and bats, be again wrapped round the female disciples of the Lord Jesus? I believe it is impossible to estimate the extent of the Church's loss, where prejudice and custom are allowed to render the outpouring of God's Spirit upon his handmaidens null and void. But it is a significant fact that in the most cold, formal, and worldly churches of the day we find least of female agency.[9]

Years later, Booth was greatly influenced by Phoebe Palmer, whom we discussed previously. When Palmer went to England, Booth was in the audience. Greatly stirred, Booth confessed before her husband's congregation that God had also called her to preach. Immediately, she started traveling. She spoke to crowds of a thousand people for seventeen consecutive weeks in Portsmouth and to twenty-five hundred who attended her meetings in Hastings.[10] Many women have been inspired by Booth's example. The Salvation Army today, in fact, is more than half women.[11]

Catherine Booth's voice still calls to us today, warning us about wasting women's gifts. Can we afford in the eleventh hour of our history "to render the outpouring of God's Spirit upon His handmaidens' null and void"? To do so means giving way to the devil, according to Franson, who said:

Two-thirds of all converted people in the world are women. . . . There is no prohibition in the Bible against women's public work, and we face the circumstance that the devil, fortunate for him, has been able to exclude nearly two-thirds of the number of Christians from participation in the Lord's service through evangelization. The loss for God's cause is so great that it can hardly be described.[12]

Part of the problem stems from a misunderstanding of the spiritual gifts God has given to all believers. Paul sums up the gifts by saying, "Follow the way of love and eagerly desire spiritual gifts, especially the gift of prophecy." And again, "Be eager to prophesy" (1 Cor 14:1, 39). In the same chapter he defines prophecy: "Everyone who prophesies speaks to men for their strengthening, encouragement and comfort" (v. 3). Three chapters earlier he specified how women are to dress when they prophesy.

My personal prayer for this gift is written in the front of my Bible. This prayer corresponds to an entry in my journal from the time in prison during World War 2 when God called me to preach the gospel. For me that call has never meant seeking ordination, but it has been linked with another call: to proclaim the priesthood of all believers—especially to women.

At the time of my call to preach the good news, I was surrounded by women preachers who were not ordained. We have referred in an earlier chapter to the great number of women who used their gifts to establish churches around the world. Most of these were not ordained. We do not see this phenomenon in the United States today because the preaching of lay ministers is not often promoted. But I write from the perspective of one who saw unordained ministers—many of whom were women—help to create the church that exists today around the world.

In the Philippines I also saw churches where men and women functioned according to their gifts, and the church experienced phenomenal growth. I have been privileged to see the gospel being preached by ordinary men and women.

The Great Commission has never changed. We are to "go and make disciples of all nations." The call and the need today is the same as when Jesus first gave the marching orders to men and women. Even though the church has been planted in most major cultures, the number of people who have not heard of God's love increases with each generation. Therefore, a great variety of ministries are needed in God's vineyard in the eleventh hour of our history. A commitment to a particular task may mean months or years or a lifetime. Men and women of all ages and almost every imaginable vocation are needed to fill posts as "tentmakers" (in countries closed to missionaries) and as professional or nonprofessional missionaries in other countries.

My daughter and her husband, for instance, have worked among Laotian refugees on the border of Thailand. She worked as an English teacher and artist, and he as a medical doctor. And serving with them were Christian men and women from the Philippines. Acts 1:8 is happening in the lives of people all over the world: You will receive power when the Holy Spirit comes upon you, and you will be my witnesses in Jerusalem (the home town), and in all Judea (the homeland) and Samaria (the neighboring country), and to the ends of the earth (the world).

But Jesus also predicted that at the close of the age "the love of most will grow cold, but she who stands firm to the end will be saved. And this gospel of the kingdom will be preached in the whole world as a testimony to all nations, and then the end will come" (Mt 24:12-14, my changes). We do not know the exact timing of the end of the age, but we do know that many today have lost their first love. Yet at the same time, the Holy Spirit is being poured out on all nations—the men and women, the rich and poor.

At the death of Christ, the curtain of the temple was torn in two. This means that instead of the priest entering the holy presence once a year, now we as a "royal priesthood" can enter God's presence every day of our lives. The priest was a man; he was a Jew and a free man. Now those qualifications are no longer necessary. The renewed priesthood embraces all the groups mentioned in Galatians 3:28: aliens, the poorest of the poor, and women. And what is

the purpose of the new priesthood? Peter says it is to "declare the praises of him who called you out of darkness into
his wonderful light" (1 Pet 2:9). We will approach God in
worship, adoration and praise, to show our gratitude for
our redemption as God's children. Then we will shout the
news of this great love from the housetops. Christ is risen!

Mary Magdalene shared this message after she had wor-
shiped the risen Christ. And before Jesus' death, Mary of
Bethany had poured costly ointment on Jesus as an act of
worship—an act so powerful that it has ministered to people
wherever the gospel has been preached. From acts like
these, spiritual children have been loved into the kingdom
of Christ.

As we open our hearts in worship to our divine Lover,
the doors for our new ministry as women will also open.
What a great age to be a woman! And in the age to come, we
will discover that the wise women of the eleventh hour "will
shine like the brightness of the heavens, and those who lead
many to righteousness, like the stars for ever and ever"
(Dan 12:3).

### Conclusion

The story is told of a Jew named Eizik, the son of Yekel, a
poor man who lived in far-off Krakow. One night Eizik had
a dream that in the distant city of Prague under a certain
bridge was hidden a treasure on the banks of the Vltava.
After the dream had recurred for two weeks, Eizik decided
to walk to Prague to look for the treasure.

A soldier found him prowling around under the bridge
and arrested him. When questioned Eizik blurted out the
story of his dream. The soldier laughed and said, "You stu-
pid Jew! Don't you know that you can't trust what you see
in dreams? Why, for the last two weeks I myself have
dreamt that faraway in Krakow, in the house of one Jew,
Eizik, son of Yekel, there is a treasure buried under the

stove in his kitchen. But wouldn't it be the most idiotic thing in the world if I were to go all the way there to look for it?"

After the soldier had given him a kick, Eizik walked back to Krakow, looked under the stove in his own kitchen and found the treasure that enabled him to live a long and fruitful life as a rich man.[13]

Most of us have ventured on similar journeys, taking the road either to the right or to the left. Like Eizik, we have not found our treasure there, but no search for truth is ever wasted. "In all things God works for the good of those who love him" (Rom 8:28). Even though I took a wrong road, the God of love turned my mistakes upside-down for my own good. Through them, he taught me to return home to my first love and find my identity in that relationship. To do so required taking the narrow path up the mountain:

How beautiful on the mountains
   are the feet of those who bring good news,
who proclaim peace,
   who bring good tidings,
   who proclaim salvation,
who say to Zion,
   "Your God reigns!" (Is 52:7)

This ancient poem foretells that as we find our identity in a love relationship with Jesus Christ, we will want to share it with others. By reaching out in love we will become prophetic voices, catalysts for change and healing agents in a hurting society. And we will continue to listen to the Voice who says,

O woman, who publishes good tiding to Zion,
   get up into the high mountain;
O woman, who publishes good tidings to Jerusalem,
   lift up your voice with strength;
Lift it up, be not afraid;
   say unto the cities of Judah,
"Behold your God." (Is 40:9, Hebrew[14])

# Notes

## Chapter 1: Introduction
[1]Paul Goodman, quoted by Patricia Meyer Spacks, *The Female Imagination* (New York: Avon Books, 1972), p. 353.
[2]Gail Sheehy, *Passages* (New York: Bantam Books, 1977), p. 208.
[3]Ibid., p. 319.
[4]*The Horse and His Boy* (New York: Macmillan, 1954), pp. 159-60. Compare this with the adoration in Rev. 5:5-10 when Christ is described as the Lion of Judah and the Lamb.

## Chapter 2: The Great Escape
[1]Betty Friedan, *The Feminine Mystique* (New York: Dell, 1963), p. 11.
[2]Ibid., p. 12.
[3]Donald Dayton, "Evangelical Roots of Feminism," unpublished paper.
[4]Helen Andelin, *Fascinating Womanhood* (Santa Barbara: Pacific Press, 1965).

## Chapter 3: Women Who Loved the Lord
[1]*Autobiography of Madame Guyon,* (Chicago: Moody Press), p. 5.
[2]Michael de la Bedoyere, *The Archbishop and the Lady* (New York: Pantheon, 1956), p. 29.
[3]Ibid., p. 31.
[4]*Madame de La Mothe Guyon* (London: Sampson Low, 1914), p. 489.
[5]Arthur F. Miller and Ralph T. Mattson, *The Truth about You* (Old Tappan, N.J.: Revell, 1977), pp. 26-27.

## Chapter 4: The Walls Come Tumbling Down
[1]Hans-Ruedi Weber, "The Gospel in the Child," *Presbyterian Outlook,* 3 Dec. 1979, p. 5.
[2]Michael Green, *Evangelism in the Early Church* (Grand Rapids, Mich.: Eerdmans, 1970), p. 216.
[3]Quoted in Green, p. 306.
[4]Ibid., p. 307.
[5]Ibid., p. 175.
[6]Virginia Mollenkott, *Women, Men, and the Bible* (Nashville: Abingdon, 1977), p. 29.
[7]David Sherman, "Woman's Place in the Gospel," in John O. Foster, *Life and Labors of Mrs. Maggie Newton Van Cott* (Cincinnati: Hitchcock and Walden, 1872), p. 34.

## Chapter 5: Women in Jesus' Day
[1]Laws about stoning women who had sexual intercourse outside of wedlock are found in Deuteronomy 22:20-30 and alluded to in John 8:4-5.

[2]Edith Dean, *The Bible's Legacy for Womanhood* (Old Tappan, N.J.: Revell, 1969), p. 223.

[3]See Helen Barrett Montgomery, *The New Testament in Modern English* (Valley Forge, Pa.: Judson Press, 1924), p. 434. In her notes on Romans 16:1-2 she says the word translated "minister" is *"diakonos,* a masculine noun, meaning 'minister' or 'servant.' See I Cor. 3:5, I Tim. 4:6, Eph. 3:7, I Thess. 3:2." The word translated "overseer" is "the Greek word prostatis.... It is the noun corresponding to the verb used in I Tim. 3:4, 5, 12. It is variously translated champion, leader, protector, patron."

[4]Dean, p. 225.

[5]*Nicene and Post-Nicene Fathers,* 14 vols. (Grand Rapids, Mich.: Eerdmans, 1975), 11:555.

[6]Quoted in Nancy Van Vuuren, *Subversion of Women As Practiced by Churches, Witch-Hunters and Other Sexists* (Philadelphia: Westminster Press, 1973), pp. 29-30.

[7]Green, p. 176.

### Chapter 6: Paul and Women

[1]Catherine Clark Kroeger and Richard Kroeger, "Pandemonium and Silence at Corinth," *The Reformed Journal,* June 1978, p. 10. Other uses of the word *laleō (lalein)* include "gossip, prattling, babbling, animal sounds and musical instrument." I am indebted to Richard and Catherine Kroeger and Berkeley and Alvera Mickelsen for their scholarly research into the basic meaning of Greek words that have influenced biblical interpretation on women's role.

[2]Plutarch, *Moralia* 505D, quoted by Richard and Catherine Kroeger in an unpublished paper.

[3]Kroeger and Kroeger, p. 9.

[4]Ibid.

[5]Quoted in Letha Scanzoni and Nancy Hardesty, *All We're Meant to Be* (Waco, Tex.: Word Books, 1974), p. 51.

[6]Quoted in Catherine Clark Kroeger and Richard Kroeger, "Sexual Identity in Corinth," *Reformed Journal,* Dec. 1978, p. 13.

[7]Jessie Penn-Lewis, *The Magna Charta of Woman* (Minneapolis: Bethany Fellowship, 1975), p. 21.

[8]Ibid., pp. 21-60.

[9]Berkeley Mickelsen, "Women in the Church," paper presented to the Baptist General Conference, Spring 1980.

[10]Richard Kroeger and Catherine Kroeger, "Ancient Heresies and a Strange Greek Verb," *Reformed Journal,* Mar. 1979, pp. 12-14.

[11]Ibid.

[12]Richard Kroeger and Catherine Kroeger, "May Women Teach?" *Reformed Journal,* Oct. 1980, p. 17.

[13]Ibid.

[14]Kroeger and Kroeger, "May Women Teach?" pp. 17-18.

[15]Green, p. 175.

[16]Martin Luther, *Commentary on Genesis*, trans. J. Theodore Mueller (Grand Rapids, Mich.: Zondervan, 1958), p. 68.

[17]Helmut Thielicke, *The Ethics of Sex*, trans. John W. Doberstein (New York: Harper & Row, 1964), p. 8.

[18]Helen B. Andelin, *Fascinating Womanhood* (Santa Barbara: Pacific Press, 1965), p. 89.

[19]A. J. Gordon, "The Ministry of Women," rpt. in *Eternity*, July-Aug. 1980, p. 31.

## Chapter 7: Leaders in the Early Church

[1]Edith Dean, p. 215.

[2]Ibid., p. 214.

[3]Edith Dean, *Great Women of the Christian Faith* (New York: Harper & Row, 1959), p. 294.

[4]Green, p. 177.

[5]Ibid., pp. 177-78.

[6]Anne Fremantle, ed., *A Treasury of Early Christianity*, (New York: Mentor Books, 1960), pp. 186-97.

[7]Lilly Lorenzen, *Of Swedish Ways* (Minneapolis: Dillon Press, 1964, p. 200.

[8]Tim Dowley, ed., *Handbook to the History of Christianity* (Grand Rapids, Mich.: Eerdmans, 1977), p. 130.

[9]Joan Morris, *The Lady Was a Bishop* (New York: Macmillan, 1973), p. 10. First published in England under the title *Hidden History*, which the author much prefers.

[10]Ibid.

[11]Ibid.

[12]From *de Virginitate*, quoted by Joan Morris in an unpublished paper.

[13]Dorothy Irvin, "The Ministry of Women in the Early Church: the Archaeological Evidence," *Duke Divinity School Review*. No. 45 (1980):79.

[14]Sister Mary Lawrence McKenna, *Women of the Church, Role and Renewal* (New York: P. J. Kennedy and Sons, 1967), p. 7.

[15]Helena Wiebe, "Women of God in Early Christian Sodalities," Fuller Theological Seminary School of World Missions, 1978, p. 7.

[16]Rosemary Ruether and Eleanor McLaughlin, *Women of Spirit* (New York: Simon and Schuster, 1979), p. 72.

[17]Gregory of Nyssa, "The Life of St. Macrina," in *Fathers of the Church*, 67 vols. (Washington: Catholic University of America), 58 (1967):167.

[18]Quoted in Edith Dean, *Great Women of the Christian Faith*, p. 12.

[19]Ibid.

[20]Ruether and McLaughlin, p. 77.

[21]Quoted in Dean, *Great Women of the Christian Faith*, p. 18.

[22]It is signifirant that when Jerome translated the Hebrew and Greek

texts into the Vulgate, which became the standard Bible for a thousand years, he had two women on his team of translators. When the New International Version was translated in the 1970s, there were no women on the committee of translators.
[23]Quoted in Dean, *Great Women of the Christian Faith*, p. 19.
[24]Ibid., p. 20.
[25]Gerontius, quoted by Ruether and McLaughlin, p. 89.
[26]Ibid., pp. 91-92. The first monastery for "chanting of continuous psalmody" is mentioned before the death of Albina and Pinion in 431-32. After Melania's trip to Constantinople in 436, she returned to Jerusalem to build another edifice for the chanting of "perpetual praises."
[27]The Venerable Bede, *A History of the English Church and People* (New York: Penguin Books, 1955), pp. 120-22.

## Chapter 8: Sustaining the Faith through the Middle Years
[1]Dean, *Great Women of the Christian Faith*, p. 35.
[2]Ibid., p. 37. For further study on the temporal and spiritual powers of abbesses in Europe, see Joan Morris, *The Lady Was a Bishop*, pp. 16-104.
[3]The Venerable Bede quoted in Dean, *Great Women of the Christian Faith*, p. 37.
[4]Dean, *Great Women of the Christian Faith*, p. 50.
[5]Ruether and McLaughlin, p. 117.
[6]Ibid., p. 118.
[7]Ibid.
[8]Ibid., p. 124.
[9]Ibid.
[10]Arthur F. Glasser, "One-half the Church—and Mission," *Women and the Ministries of Christ*, ed. Roberta Hestenes and Lois Curly (Pasadena: Fuller Theological Seminary, 1978), p. 91.
[11]John Calvin's reply to friends who had urged him to marry. Quoted in Dean, *Great Women of the Christian Faith*, p. 322.
[12]Norman Penney, ed., *First Publishers of Truth* (London: Headley Brothers, 1907), p. 87.
[13]George Fox, *Journal*, rev. Norman Penney (New York: Dutton, 1924), pp. 14-15.
[14]Maria Webb, *The Fells of Swarthmore Hall* (Philadelphia: Longstreth, 1884), pp. 29-30.
[15]Dean, *Great Women of the Christian Faith*, pp. 126-27.
[16]Ibid.
[17]Norman Penney, pp. 258-59.
[18]Quoted in Hope Elizabeth Luder, *Women and Quakerism* (Pendle Hill, 1974), p. 6.
[19]Emily Manners, *Elizabeth Hooten: First Quaker Woman Preacher* (Lon-

don: Headley Brothers, 1914), p. 41.

[20]Dean, *Great Women of the Christian Faith,* pp. 128-29.

[21]Ibid., p. 142.

[22]Susannah Wesley in a letter to her husband. Quoted by Della Olson, *A Woman of Her Times* (Minneapolis: Free Church Press, 1977), pp. 86-87.

[23]Donald Dayton, "Women in American Evangelicalism," *Radix* (Jan./ Feb. 1979), p. 9.

[24]Ibid., p. 14.

[25]Quoted in Dayton, p. 9.

[26]Dean, *Great Women of the Christian Faith,* p. 152.

[27]Ibid.

[28]Ibid., p. 154.

## Chapter 9: Building Christianity in the New World

[1]Nancy Hardesty, Lucille Sider Dayton and Donald W. Dayton, "Women in the Holiness Movement: Feminism in the Evangelical Tradition," in Ruether and McLaughlin, p. 226.

[2]Phoebe Palmer, *Promise of the Father* (Boston: Henry V. Degen, 1859), p. 341.

[3]Ibid., p. 7.

[4]Ibid., p. 347.

[5]V. Raymond Edman, *Finney Lives On* (Wheaton, Ill.: Scripture Press, 1951), p. 15.

[6]Ibid., p. 59.

[7]Bennet Tyler, quoted by Hardesty, Dayton and Dayton, p. 230.

[8]Theodore Weld, quoted in Gilbert Barnes and Dwight Dumond, eds., *Letters of Theodore Dwight Weld, Angeline Grimke Weld and Sarah Grimke, 1822-44,* vol. 1 (Gloucester, Mass.: Peter Smith, 1965), p. 432.

[9]Edman, p. 137.

[10]Charles Grandison Finney, *Memoirs* (New York: A. S. Barnes & Co., 1870), p. 443.

[11]Ray Strachey, *Frances Willard: Her Life and Work* (New York: Revell, 1913), p. 209.

[12]Ibid., p. 208.

[13]Amanda Smith, *An Autobiography: The Story of the Lord's Dealing with Amanda Smith* (Nobelsville, Ind.: Newby Book Room, 1972, original edition, 1893), p. 185.

[14]Ibid., p. 211.

[15]Ibid., p. vi.

[16]Timothy L. Smith, *Called unto Holiness* (Kansas City: Nazarene Publishing House, 1962), p. 155.

[17]Seth Cook Rees, *The Ideal Pentecostal Church* (Cincinnati: M. W. Knapp, 1897), p. 41.

[18]Paul S. Rees, *Seth Cook Rees: The Warrior Saint* (Indianapolis: Pilgrim

Book Room, 1934), p. 13.

[19]Melvin Easterday Dieter, "Revivalism and Holiness," Ph.D. dissertation, Temple University, 1972, p. 50.

[20]Mrs. P. L. U. (Phoebe L. Upham), "Woman's Freedom in Worship," *Guide to Holiness*, vol. 43 (April-May 1863):114-15.

[21]Sadie J. Hart, "My Experience," *Guide to Holiness*, vol. 6 (April 1869): 114-15.

[22]Richard Wheatley, *The Life and Letters of Mrs. Phoebe Palmer* (New York: W. C. Palmer, Jr., 1876), p. 283.

[23]J. Fowler Willing, "Woman and the Pentecost," *Guide to Holiness*, vol. 68 (January 1898):21.

[24]Hardesty, Dayton and Dayton, p. 250. Much of the material in this section comes from their chapter on "Women in the Holiness Movement," in *Women of Spirit*, ed. Ruether and McLaughlin.

[25]Ethel Ruff, *When the Saints Go Marching* (New York: Exposition Press, 1957), pp. 77-85.

[26]Olson, p. 64.

[27]Quoted in Olson, p. 67.

[28]Ibid., p. 69.

[29]Ibid., p. 72.

[30]Ibid., p. 82.

[31]Donald W. Dayton, "Evangelical Roots of Feminism," (mimeographed paper, Chicago), p. 14.

**Chapter 10: Ministering as Single Women**

[1]Scanzoni and Hardesty, p. 146.

[2]Augustine quoted in Patricia Gundry, *Heirs Together* (Grand Rapids Mich.: Zondervan, 1980), p. 49.

[3]*So You're Single*, quoted in *Bookshorts*, Dec.-Jan. 1978-79, p. 98.

[4]R. Pierce Beaver, *All Loves Excelling* (Grand Rapids, Mich.: Eerdmans, 1968), p. 107.

[5]Ibid., pp. 109, 116.

[6]Ibid., p. 108.

[7]William G. Lennox, *The Health and Turnover of Missionaries* (New York. Foreign Missions Conference of North America, 1933), p. 28.

[8]Helen Barrett Montgomery, *Western Women in Eastern Lands* (New York: Macmillan, 1910), pp. 243-44.

[9]Information in a letter of 12 May 1981 to the author from Jane K. Mees who quotes Dr. Ralph Winter of the U. S. Center for World Mission.

[10]*Mission Handbook*, quoted in R. Pierce Beaver, *American Protestant Women in World Mission* (Grand Rapids, Mich.: Eerdmans, 1980), p. 216.

[11]Beaver, *All Loves Excelling*, pp. 200-02.

[2]Malcolm Muggeridge, *Something Beautiful for God* (Garden City, N.Y.: Image Books, 1971), p. 37.

[13]Joan Morris, p. 7.

[14]Herbert J. Miles, *Sexual Understanding before Marriage* (Grand Rapids, Mich.: Zondervan, 1971), p. 177.

[15]Scanzoni and Hardesty, p. 145.

[16]Dave and Neta Jackson have written *Living Together in a World Falling Apart* (Carol Stream, Ill.: Creation House, 1974), an excellent handbook on Christian community; and *Coming Together* (Minneapolis: Bethany Fellowship, 1978), where they go into more detail and list all the existing communities in the United States.

## Chapter 11: Interacting as Married Women

[1]Paul K. Jewett, *Man as Male and Female* (Grand Rapids, Mich.: Eerdmans, 1975), p. 36.

[2]Berkeley and Alvera Mickelsen, "Biblical Teachings about Men-Women Relationships," course outline for classes taught in churches in the Minneapolis-St. Paul area, p. 2.

[3]Ibid.

[4]Walter Trobisch, *My Wife Made Me a Polygamist* (Downers Grove, Ill.: InterVarsity Press, 1971), pp. 47-48.

[5]*Paradise Lost* 4. 288-92, 318-22.

[6]Ibid. 1. 1-3.

[7]Ibid. 1. 98.

[8]Patricia Gundry, pp. 87-88.

[9]*A Doll's House,* trans. Farquharson Sharp and Eleanor Marx-Aveling (New York: Dutton, 1958), pp. 67-68.

[10]Bob Mumford, *Living Happily Ever After* (Old Tappan, N.J.: Revell, 1973), pp. 29-30, 45.

[11]*A Christian View of Men's and Women's Roles in a Changing World* (Family '76 Incorporated, 1975), p. 20.

[12]Marabel Morgan, *The Total Woman* (Old Tappan, N.J.: Revell, 1973), p. 80.

[13]Judith Miles, *The Feminine Principle: A Woman's Discovery of the Key to Total Fulfillment* (Minneapolis: Bethany Fellowship, 1975), p. 44, italics mine.

[14]*Paradise Regained* 4. 613-15, 633-35.

[15]Berkeley and Alvera Mickelsen, pp. 10-13. The Mickelsens point out that "only *8 times* out of approximately 180 times does the Septuagint use the literal word *kephale* (head) to translate the Hebrew word *ro'sh.* Why? Translators recognize that *kephale* (head) did not normally in Greek mean 'leader.' So except for 8 times they used 13 clearer words when the Old Testament passages meant leader."

[16]Watchman Nee, *The Normal Christian Life* (London: Witness and Testimony Publishers, 1958), pp. 196-200. It is interesting to note that this Chinese Christian sees Paul's allusion to Genesis 2, before sin came into the world, as an aspect of Calvary that had nothing to do with sin. God

wanted a church, and brought one out of Christ's wounded side.
[17]Jewett, p. 140.

## Chapter 12: Making Christ the Head of the Home
[1]From *Cabaret*, lyrics by Fred Ebb, quoted in *The Equal Rights Monitor*, May-June 1977, p. 3.
[2]Cathy Guisewite, "Cathy," *The Equal Rights Monitor*, May-June 1977, p. 5.
[3]*Rich Christians in an Age of Hunger* (Downers Grove, Ill.: InterVarsity Press, 1977), p. 111.
[4]Another good study for households that are exploring the possibilities of what God might ask them to do is the book *Cry Justice: The Bible on Hunger and Poverty*, edited by Ron Sider (Downers Grove, Ill.: Inter-Varsity Press, 1980). We can also be provoked to action by the writings of Third-World leaders like C. René Padilla of Ecuador who said, "The poverty of the Third World places a question mark over the lifestyle of people, and particularly of Christians, in the West. And the proper response to it, to begin with, is a simple lifestyle and a radical restructuring of the economic relationships among Christians everywhere, based on the Biblical concept of stewardship" ("The Fullness of Missions," *Occasional Bulletin*, no. 3 [Jan. 1979], p. 9).

## Chapter 13: Sharing Christ in Society
[1]Katie Curin, *Women in China* (New York: Pathfinder Press, 1975), p. 10.
[2]John MacArthur quoted in Norman B. Rohrer, "Reversing the Curse," *Christianity Today*, 6 April 1979, pp. 46-47.
[3]Marie Monsen, *The Awakening*, trans. Joy Guinness (London: China Inland Mission, 1961), pp. 35-36.
[4]See Rebecca Manley Pippert, *Out of the Saltshaker* (Downers Grove, Ill.: InterVarsity Press, 1979), a book on evangelism written by a woman.
[5]C. S. Lewis, *The Screwtape Letters* (Grand Rapids, Mich.: Baker Book House, 1969), p. 51.
[6]Gail Sheehy, pp. 379-80.
[7]Ibid., p. 319.
[8]Arthur Miller and Ralph Mattson, *The Truth about You* (Old Tappan, N.J.: Revell, 1977).

## Chapter 14: Women in the Eleventh Hour
[1]Edvard P. Torjesen, unpublished manuscript on the life of Fredrik Franson.
[2]Robert E. Coleman, *Songs of Heaven* (Old Tappan, N.J.: Revell, 1980), p. 117.
[3]According to the *American Heritage Dictionary*, preaching means "To

expand upon in writing or speech; especially, to urge acceptance of or compliance with (specified religious or moral principles)."

[4]Elizabeth O'Connor, *Eighth Day of Creation* (Waco, Tex.: Word, 1971), pp. 42-43.

[5]Stephen B. Clark, *Spiritual Gifts* (Pecos, N.M.: Dove Publications, 1969), p. 23.

[6]Fredrik Franson, *Prophesying Daughters,* trans. Vernon Mortenson, The Evangelical Alliance Mission, Wheaton, Ill., unpublished, p. 19.

[7]Ibid.

[8]F. De. L. Booth-Tucker, *The Life of Catherine Booth* (New York: Revell, 1892), chap. 12, p. 82.

[9]Quoted in Lucille Sider Dayton, "The Rise of Women in Evangelicalism," unpublished article.

[10]Booth-Tucker, p. 244.

[11]Lareta Halteman Finger, "Women in the Pulpit," *The Other Side,* 94 (July 1979), p. 20.

[12]Franson, p. 2.

[13]Belden C. Lane, "Rabbinical Stories: A Primer on Theological Method," *The Christian Century,* 16 Dec. 1981, p. 1309.

[14]This translation follows the alternate reading in the RSV and the primary reading in the NIV. In these readings the herald (the one addressed) must be assumed to be feminine because of the feminine participles and verbs in the Hebrew.